Conquering Our Unseen Enemies

Understand Satan's Tactics and Overcome Demonic Influences

Dawn Simmons

Cover Photo by: Chris Linnett

DEDICATION

I want to dedicate this to my husband, Don. His constant support and encouragement seem to know no bounds. No matter what I have going on or what direction I need to go, he is always there to cheer me on and provide whatever support is required. He makes everything fun and adventurous.

Acknowledgements

I want to acknowledge the women in my life who have come around and encircled me with encouragement and support. They have enriched my life in ways they don't fully understand. My original SALO ladies!
Erica
Eva
Sue
Jacinta
Jenni
Hannah D.
Rocio

Table of Contents

Introduction

I want to take start first by giving you a rundown of what we are going to be examining during this journey of **Conquering Our Unseen Enemies**. Understand it is a journey, not a race. Our purpose together here is to gain an understanding of the spirit realm and learn to develop spiritual discernment to enable us in **Conquering Our Unseen Enemies** once and for all. To be successful in our journey, we must understand what and how and why behind our experiences in order to truly make the changes needed to eliminate demonic influences in our lives and those around us. I'm going to let you know now, where we are going together is considered controversial. For some, discussing demons is scary, for some, these topics should be off limits, and we should only focus on the light of the world and pay no attention to the dark. Jesus spent quite a bit of His time explaining to us about how the enemy, the dark, Satan, our Accuser, works so the more we understand, the better equipped we are to conquer what is interfering in our lives. As we continue, I will be sharing stories of how to develop spiritual discernment and experiences with both the Kingdom of God and the kingdom of Satan. We will go deep into understanding how Satan works, and answer questions like how do demons group? How do demons enter people? What are the strategies they use to attack us? How we can overcome their attacks? We will look at 14 specific demons which are well known influencers in our lives. Lastly, we will focus on developing an understanding of the weapons we have available to us as believers.

So why do I, as a believer, want to even address these issues? The misguided will say that we should not focus on such things and doing so gives the enemy power. Well, by exposing how Satan works so we can begin to exercise the authority the Bible says we already have is, by its very nature, focusing on the Kingdom of God. Where we, as the body of Christ, need to go is to a place where we no longer fear the devil like he is the big bad wolf or see him as a red cartoon character we joke about. We, as a church, need to go to a place where our discernment enables us to see, know and understand what he truly is, what his demons are doing and how we can get their influence out of our lives. Eliminating demonic influence will reduce conflict and chaos and clear your path for a better life. As we progress, you will hear stories you may not believe, at least not at first. The deeper we go, the more we will expose the lies and deception the enemy consistently uses against us. There is so much darkness out there in the world. Together we can position you to be able to rid the enemy of his influence over you.

Before we step out and begin our journey, I want to lay out a few ground rules for us:

First and foremost, all that we discuss is grounded in the Word. We have scriptural references for the Biblical principles we are applying in our discussions.

Second, we will be discussing a lot of demonic activity, but our focus is how to defeat the devil. We are not so focused on demons that we see a demon around every corner. Demons are not responsible for every bad thing that happens to us, sometimes our negative consequences are a result of bad choices. So, we aren't going in with a victim mentality and everything is the not the devil's fault.

Third, these issues we discuss are black and white – literally and figuratively. There is no gray. We are not to be like the church in Laodicea, lukewarm, where we get spit out of the Lord's mouth.

Fourth, these issues we will be discussing are polarizing in the Christian community. Because we are grounded in the Bible, we are grounded in Truth.

Fifth and finally, this is a challenging area to address in our lives. Stepping into this is real and you will find out more about yourself than you realized. We will do this together, and this journey will strengthen you and develop your Spiritual discernment in ***Conquering Our Unseen Enemies.***

Are you ready?

Conquering Our Unseen Enemies

Part One:

Two Eternal Kingdoms at Work

Chapter 1

Two Kingdoms

To go into all of the places we will need for **Conquering Our Unseen Enemies**, we need to create our foundation and clarify the worlds in which we are living. We have a natural world and a spiritual world. These worlds have two kingdoms.

The first is the Kingdom of God or the Kingdom of Light

People living in this Kingdom are believers. We have our salvation in Jesus and this kingdom is built on the Word of God, Truth. Those living in this kingdom know where they are because it is light, they can see. Anyone who is a citizen of God's Kingdom is automatically at war with the kingdom of Satan and most don't even know it. This Kingdom is everlasting, and it is the place from where God and Jesus rule forevermore.

In terms of where it is located, we'll start with referencing Genesis 1:1, which states "*in the beginning God created the heavens and the earth.*" Notice it says God created the heavens, plural so we know that the Kingdom of God functions in more than one area, and that God created these areas. Paul describes Jesus' ascension in Ephesians 4:10 and again describes heavens in the plural. In 2 Corinthians 12:2, Paul tells us "*he knew a man caught up in the third heaven.*" In 1 Kings

8:27, King Solomon is speaking to God and also talks of multiple heavens "*The heavens, even the highest heaven, cannot contain you.*" And again, in verse 35 referring to "*the heavens shut up,*" referring to a lack of rain. So, from this we know that there are at least three heavens in which God's kingdom functions. We will dig into this more when we discuss battles the Bible describes but for our purposes here understand that there are three levels of heaven revealed to us in scripture.

So, who has access to these heavenlies? Based on Daniel 10, we can see that both God's Kingdom and Satan's kingdom have access to at least one of the heavens. The Angel appearing to Daniel describes a battle with the prince of the Persian Kingdom. The Angel further tells Daniel he was held back from responding to Daniel's prayer sooner by the King of Persia. The battle was so difficult, that Michael, one of the chief princes, another Angel from God's kingdom, had to come to help him. So, in this we also hear about the structure of the kingdoms. There is a hierarchy with the Angels and both God's Kingdom and Satan's Kingdom have access to at least one level of the heavens at the same time. Another place we can gain some understanding of the heavens is in Job 1:6. The scripture says "*One day the angels came to present themselves before the Lord, and Satan also came with them. The Lord said to Satan, "Where have you come from?" Satan answered the Lord, "From roaming throughout the earth, going back and forth on it."*

This scripture is huge for us, we gain an understanding of Satan's activities and a hint at his objective. So, let's examine the Kingdom of Satan.

The Kingdom of Satan is a kingdom of darkness, deception, people cannot see truth in this kingdom. Jesus tells us in

Luke 10:18 that he *"saw Satan fall like lightning from heaven."* When Jesus says this, he is referring to Isaiah 14:12 "*How you have fallen from heaven, morning star, son of the dawn! You have been cast down to the earth, you who once laid low the nations!"* So, this tells us that the Kingdom of Satan is a created kingdom, created by God originally before the fall where Satan was cast out of heaven. When Satan was cast out, the angels under him fell with him. Revelation 12:4 reveals that one third of the angels went with Satan in the fall which are now what we refer to as demons. So now we know the size of the Kingdom of Darkness in relation to the Kingdom of God. In John 10:10, Jesus tells us the objective of Satan: *"The thief comes only to steal and kill and destroy; I have come that they may have life and have it to the full."* Believers can participate in this kingdom even though they are citizens of God's kingdom, sometimes it is by choice in turning from God; other times it is in ignorance as a result of falling for Satan's deception.

So now comes the question, in which kingdom do you spend your time? I certainly hope you said the Kingdom of God, but the truth is even though we live in the Kingdom of God, we are influenced daily by the Kingdom of Darkness. Some influences are obvious and those can be pretty easy to avoid, but it's the subtle, deceptive, disguised influences that get us into the most trouble. This is where the Kingdom of Darkness will try to cloud issues and make what's dark appear grey, or even worse, deceive us enough to think darkness is light.

As we progress, we will breakdown the strategies and tactics of the kingdom of darkness and reveal the truth so that we know how to get out of dark situations, and also how to recognize deception as it approaches you. The challenge in doing this is not to become so obsessed with hunting down demons, destroying idols or, letting fear grip you. Fear can prevent you receiving the information you need to be able to grow in understanding and wisdom. Similarly, when we become obsessive, even if it is for the right reason, it will create an obstacle to your growth. We need to remain balanced and open to the promptings of the Holy Spirit, and we need to remain consistent in the Word, which is our source. If you don't have a consistent Bible reading schedule, now is a great time to start one. Spiritual discernment cannot be developed without it.

In Ephesians 4:27, the Bible tells us "*never give a place to the devil.*" Well, if we leave the devil alone, we are permitting him to continue his deception completely unchallenged. The result is more people will be brought down into his world. More lives will be lost through suicide or drug addiction; more marriages ripped apart through adultery or domestic violence; more violent crimes will tear our communities apart and terrorize innocent people, more - well you know all the terrible things we have in this world; we hear about it daily in the news. It doesn't have to be this way. For some, it will, unfortunately, because they choose that path even after being given an opportunity to know the truth. But for others, gaining understanding and wisdom in Satan's tactics can be the difference between a life of misery or a life free of bondage. Satan is all about bondage. As long as he can keep us suspended in unbelief or prevent us from understanding we have authority over him or even challenging us so we won't use that authority, he will beat us every time.

Bad theology perpetuates common misconceptions among believers that keeps Satan in business so to speak. One of those misconceptions is the belief that if we have enough

faith, God will automatically take care of demons. Maybe calling that a misconception was not the right word, it is actually a lie. It's a lie Satan wants us to believe but Jesus told us otherwise. In Matthew 10:1, Jesus gave his disciples *"authority to drive our impure spirits and heal every disease and sickness."* It is repeated in Luke 9:1, and in Mark 16:17, Jesus says "*Whoever believes and is baptized will be saved, but whoever does not believe will be condemned. And these signs will accompany those who believe: In my name they will drive out demons; they will speak in new tongues; they will pick up snakes with their hands; and when they drink deadly poison, it will not hurt them at all; they will place their hands on sick people, and they will get well."*

As believers, **we** have been given both the authority and the responsibility to rid ourselves of demons. If we were not able to do so, Jesus would not have left us here alone to fend for ourselves. He gave his life for us, so he clearly cares for our wellbeing. He gave us what we need to take care of the devil ourselves, not to rely on God to do the work for us. To be passive and not take a stand and confront Satan's deceptions and tactics in our lives will keep us in bondage. **Faith** does become integral in this process by **believing** in the authority we have received from Jesus, in **acting** on that authority in the name of Jesus and in **trusting** in that authority to take care of the problem in Jesus' name. So, we are required to act, and have faith in our action, but the power is in the name of Jesus. Jesus gave us authority to use, and we need to use it, not expect someone else to do it for us.

We will talk much more about authority as we progress, but I wanted to at least lay some groundwork here, so we are all in the same starting point. We will be building our knowledge and understanding in each chapter.

13

As we continue in each chapter, we are also going to clear up misconceptions, lies, myths, whatever we want to call them. This is really important to get these out of our way because they can interfere with you being able to apply Biblical wisdom and understanding. When we carry manmade religious beliefs that are not based on the Bible, those beliefs will counteract the truth the bible reveals about Satan's tactics. That is exactly how Satan works to keep us confused.

Many churches do not teach on the topics we will cover. The denominational church I was raised in didn't address the spirit realm or the Holy Spirit. Not teaching the body of Christ about the Holy Spirit is robbing the body of the head. Not teaching the body of Christ that *"we do not wrestle against flesh and blood"* is equally disastrous. Jesus never told us that demons will disappear and cease to be when He ascends. To the contrary, we know that if we read the Book of Revelation that there is warfare to come. The Spiritual realm was there in the beginning when God created everything, and it will be there throughout eternity, so we need to understand it is in existence today where we are right now. We may not know when Satan was thrown down from heaven, but we know he is still roaming the earth, so we have work to do.

We will talk about ways demons enter, we will address discernment, explain strongholds and how we defeat the strongman. We will also breakdown how demons group together and how demon groups function. We will discuss fourteen demons specifically and the tools used in tearing us down to enable and position these demons to get rooted in our thoughts. Once they get rooted in our thoughts, then they move to our hearts and attack us from the inside. We

14

need to get this darkness in the open, into the light and understand it through the Holy Spirit giving us discernment, wisdom and understanding.

Chapter 2

The Great I Am vs Satan

When we are in the midst of a battle or even just trying to understand what is going on around us, remembering the names as God as He refers to Himself and applying those names in our situation will help us to discern what could be at the root of our situation. From that discernment, you will know how to move through your situation with Him. If we are going to be **Conquering Our Unseen Enemies**, we need to understand what is at the core of our unseen enemy.

When we look at names in the Bible, names are revealing in nature and character. For example, we read Jesus is referred to as the "Messiah" which means "The Anointed One." The name Daniel means "God is My Judge." In Genesis we read that God changed Abram's name to Abraham which means "father of multitudes or father of nations." God changed Abram's name because God was revealing who Abram was to become. Names are important in the Bible for other reasons as well. Through names, we see how the name of a person can represent their relationship to us. A name reveals character. A name reveals purpose. A name reveals past, present and future.

Let's start looking at how God began to reveal His character and relationship to us in Exodus.

Exodus 3: 1-5, *Now Moses was tending the flock of Jethro his father-in-law, the priest of Midian, and he led the flock to the far side of the*

17

*wilderness and came to Horeb, the mountain of God. There the angel of the LORD appeared to him in **flames of fire from within a bush. Moses saw that though the bush was on fire it did not burn up**. So Moses thought, "I will go over and see this strange sight— why the bush does not burn up." When the LORD saw that he had gone over to look, God called to him from within the bush, "Moses! Moses!" And Moses said, "Here I am." "Do not come any closer," God said. "Take off your sandals, for **the place where you are standing is holy ground**." Then he said, "**I am the God of your father, the God of Abraham, the God of Isaac and the God of Jacob**." At this, Moses hid his face, because he was afraid to look at God.*

We can already see from just this part of the exchange between them how God is willing at times to show Himself to us in a way that we cannot comprehend. The bush that did not burn went against what Moses knew to be logical in this world. From this we know, God will work wonders for our benefit. We also see from this exchange that the ground where God is presenting himself is holy, therefore God is holy. Then God introduces himself. He tells Moses who He is; He does not hide it; He is specific and puts it in terms Moses will understand and identify with.

As we read on, we see God is calling Moses to leave this wilderness and His flock and instead go back to Egypt and lead the Israelites out of Egypt. Moses is giving him some pushback. I am sure we would all react that way when you imagine the enormity of the task for Moses to complete.

Back to Verse 11, But *Moses said to God, "Who am I that I should go to Pharaoh and bring the Israelites out of Egypt?" [12] And God said, "**I will be with you**.* (so again, God is revealing to Moses a characteristic of who God is) *And this will be the sign to you that*

*it is I who have sent you: When you have brought the people out of Egypt, you will worship God on this mountain." Moses said to God, "Suppose I go to the Israelites and say to them, 'The God of your fathers has sent me to you,' and they ask me, 'What is his name?' Then what shall I tell them?" God said to Moses, "***I AM WHO I AM***. This is what you are to say to the Israelites: '***I AM*** has sent me to you.'" God also said to Moses, "Say to the Israelites, 'The* LORD **the God of your fathers—the God of Abraham, the God of Isaac and the God of Jacob**—*has sent me to you.'*
*"This is **my name forever**,*
the name you shall call me
from generation to generation.

From this part of their discussion again God is telling Moses who He is in relation to Moses by bringing in Abraham, Isaac and Jacob and in relation to the Israelites. Moses knows who his descendants are; he knows he is an Israelite, so Moses can identify with this and God's people. He also tells Moses, I Am who I Am. He says, I Am sent you. It's simple yet so profound--- He just is. We'll dig into that deeper, but remember that, I Am. Now let's backtrack a minute and see what happened before Moses. Why did Moses know who God was in relation to Abraham, Isaac and Jacob?

Genesis 15:1, After this, the word of the LORD came to Abram in a vision:

"Do not be afraid, Abram.
*I am your **shield**,*
*your very **great reward**."*

God is revealing Himself to Abram and sets the stage as to what Abram can expect from Him. This is the beginning of God creating His people. God must introduce Himself to

19

Abram so God can begin to build Abram into the man He created Him to be, the father of the nation of Israel and ultimately the lineage from which Jesus will be born. What God reveals to Abram is still the same for us today, He is our shield and our great reward. When you are having a moment. When you are needing comfort, just call on His name, I Am. He knows what you are going through, He will be there.

Let's go spend some time with Isaiah.

*Isaiah 43:3, For **I am the LORD your God,**
the **Holy One of Israel**, your **Savior;***

Again, He says, I Am and then tells us specifically who He is and what that means in relation to us.

Isaiah 43: 5, Do *not be afraid, for I am with you;*

Another I Am, and a reassurance for us that He is here with us through everything.

Isaiah 43: 10, ***Before me no god was formed,
nor will there be one after** me.
I, even I, am the LORD,
and **apart from me there is no savior.***

Here God is telling us, who He is in relation to everything and everyone else. Then again, letting us know our place in relation to Him with a very definitive description of our place with Him.

Isaiah 43: 12, *You are my witnesses," declares the* LORD, *"that I am God.
Yes, and from **ancient days I am he.***

No one can deliver out of my hand.
When I act, who can reverse it?"

This verse tells us a lot, but I want to touch on I Am again for a minute. He refers to Himself as I Am throughout the Bible, and then in the New Testament - Jesus does as well. The reason I like this so much is that it speaks of Him as yesterday, today and forever. He never changes. In Malachi 3, we read "I, the Lord do not change." We read in Hebrews 13:8 that He is the same yesterday, today and forever. When He says I Am, there is no limitation. It's not, I used to be but now I am this. There is no, someday I will be, but for now I am this. When we read words written thousands of years ago that mean the same today and will mean the same to our children's children, it truly reveals, He is I Am.

One of my favorite references to Him is Ancient Days or Ancient One depending on the translation. He always has, and He always will be. We cannot fathom how long He has been I Am because there is no beginning and no end in His existence. When he says "no one can deliver out of my hand" that tells us that He controls everything, and the place we want to be is in His hand. Let's keep going.

Isaiah 64:4, *Since ancient times no one has heard,*
no ear has perceived,
no eye has seen any God besides you,
who acts on behalf of those who wait for him.

This again explains who God is in relation to us, but also tells us something about who He is in providing for us. He "acts on behalf of those who wait for Him." There is a two-way communication here. That implies relationship. He wants us to have a relationship; He created us with that as His

21

objective, and He expects us to be in relationship with Him so that He can act for us, in place of us, so that whatever He does is right and true. It also tells us our position in Him. At times, we will need to give to Him our issues, let Him work them out, submit to His plan over the situation and wait for Him to resolve it His way on our behalf.

Isaiah 64: 8, *Yet you, LORD, are our Father.*
 We are the clay, you are the potter;
 we are all the work of your hand.

This is the perfect analogy for accepting who He is in relation to us. Again, we want to be in His hands, and if we allow ourselves to be the clay and He is the potter shaping us into what He creates us to be, then we will be perfect in His eyes for what He created us to do.

While we could spend hours on who God is, we are going to end our discussion of God with this last verse from Daniel 7:13, *"In my vision at night I looked, and there before me was one like a son of man,[a] coming with the clouds of heaven. He approached the* **Ancient of Days** *and was led into his presence.*

Daniel is describing this and in Daniel's description which is "God breathed," he refers to God as Ancient of Days, the same way God refers to Himself. Daniel is also talking of Jesus, so we see the two together, and we begin to see their relationship. Jesus is able to approach God and be in His presence. That is an important detail to know because Jesus does that very same thing on our behalf against the accuser which is what we are discussing next.

Satan has many names: Prince of Darkness, Beelzebub, the Antichrist, Father of Lies, Ancient Serpent. All names of which he lives up, but too often we forget all the ways he works to live up to his names.

Let's start with Revelation 12;10, *Then I heard a loud voice in heaven say:*
"Now have come the salvation and the power
 and the kingdom of our God,
 and the authority of his Messiah.
For the accuser of our brothers and sisters,
 who accuses them before our God day and night,
 has been hurled down.

We can never forget the accuser, Satan, and his demonic beings are present, and the purpose of their presence is to trick us and deceive us into doing what is against God. Once we fail to recognize the trick and we fall prey to their deception, Satan then goes to God and accuses us of doing what his demons set in place as traps for us. By failing to recognize the trick and falling prey to their deception, by default, we come into agreement with the enemy and that gives Satan permission to evoke a penalty against us. It's just as if we were in an earthly court of law being accused of wrongdoing. Jesus acts as our attorney, defending us against the Accuser. We see in Job how Satan himself tells what his objective is in the world. Job 1:6, *One day the angels came to present themselves before the* LORD, *and Satan also came with them. The* LORD *said to Satan, "Where have you come from?"*

Satan answered the LORD, *"From roaming throughout the earth, going back and forth on it."*

1 Peter 5:8 tells us what he is doing while he is roaming, *"Be alert and of sober mind. Your enemy the devil prowls around like a roaring lion looking for someone to devour."*

23

Let's look at a few more places that tell us who Satan is and that reveal who he is in relation to us.

Revelation 20:10: *And the devil, who deceived them, was thrown into the lake of burning sulfur, where the beast and the false prophet had been thrown. They will be tormented day and night for ever and ever.*

His character is revealed as a deceiver and as a result, in the end times, he will pay the price for all he has done, and he will pay that price forever and ever.

Matthew 4:1, *Then Jesus was led by the Spirit into the wilderness to be tempted by the devil. ² After fasting forty days and forty nights, he was hungry. ³ The tempter came to him and said, "If you are the Son of God, tell these stones to become bread."*

We can see from this exchange; Satan was tempting Jesus while He was in the wilderness. Temptation is a very common tactic of Satan. If Satan was working to try to tempt Jesus away from serving God, His own Father, why wouldn't we think Satan would also use this same tactic against us? All too often we allow ourselves to be put into a position where we know there will be temptation, and we brush it off, or even worse justify it, and down the road end up in sinful situations we never should have taken part in, and we knew it. Instead, we allowed Satan to convince us it's not that big of a deal. Many marriages have been destroyed because of deceit that starts with Satan tempting us; and then we come into agreement with it and start using it on ourselves to justify and endorse bad behavior.

24

Isaiah 13: 12-16,

How you have fallen from heaven,
morning star, son of the dawn!
You have been cast down to the earth,
you who once laid low the nations!
[13] You said in your heart,
"I will ascend to the heavens;
I will raise my throne
above the stars of God;
I will sit enthroned on the mount of assembly,
on the utmost heights of Mount Zaphon.[h]
[14] I will ascend above the tops of the clouds;
I will make myself like the Most High."
[15] But you are brought down to the realm of the dead,
to the depths of the pit.

This reveals to us who Satan has at the center of everything - himself. His purposes are to serve himself, and that means he wants to draw us away from God to serve him and his purposes. A sharp contrast to what God reveals of Himself to us.

Lucifer and some of the names we have for Satan are a result of translations. For example, Lucifer came as a result of an early Latin translation called the Vulgate. Knowing that the name, Lucifer, is associated or speaks specifically of Satan, we need to consider that when we see that name used anywhere else. There is a TV show right now that is called Lucifer. I have never watched it, nor will I ever watch it. The marketing of it is depicted in reds, oranges, yellows and black. It is done in a way that subtly indicates some ties or reference to Satan as mankind has come to depict him. Whatever the show is about, the marketing of it is aligning itself with how we perceive Satan, so that would be something that my discernment would tell me to avoid. Why? Not because I am afraid of a show. There is nothing the show itself can do to me, though I doubt it would hold my interest. The reason is that by knowingly and intentionally watching something that is purposefully aligning itself with Lucifer, I am, in essence, opening a door to other things that are also aligned or associated with Lucifer. It would be subtle, somewhat like the marketing, but then slowly become less and less subtle. Over time I will have positioned myself to allow the enemy to have influence in my life. Once there is influence, authority comes in and is legally allowed to move in my life.

If you are shaking your head thinking, "all of that as a result of watching a TV show? Yes, all of that as a result of watching a show. The tactic is to move in quietly, so you don't even realize it and then spread. It's a cancer. The things of this world, the things of Satan, are a cancer to everyone, believers and unbelievers alike. We turn a blind eye to it thinking it is harmless and the next thing you know, Stage 4 and need help.

The name Satan in Hebrew is translated as adversary or accuser. By using specific names, God is revealing to us what we can expect from Satan and those who work for him. When we name someone, that isn't always the case. For example, my name is Dawn, which means the first appearance of light, daybreak. This is not when you want to see me. I am not naturally one of those people who walks into work all "Good morning!" All smiles. No, I have to work at that. The funny thing is, I must have taught my parrot "good morning," because while I am still in bed, I can hear him up at dawn, literally, and he is looking out his window yelling "Good morning!" He has several different variations of 'Good Morning.' I know it is because he hears me say it differently. It's pretty funny, if you want to know what you sound like and what phrases you use frequently, get a parrot. You learn a little about yourself. Anyhow, my point is, God names things for what they are or will become; we tend to name things for our own reasons that may or may not have anything to do with what we are or will become.

This next scripture is Jesus talking about who Satan is, and it screams of telling us what we can expect from Satan. This is Jesus talking to the Pharisees, who were the religious leaders of the day who became corrupted by Satan. John 8:44, *You belong to your father, the devil, and you want to carry out your father's desires. He was a murderer from the beginning, not holding to the truth, for there is no truth in him. When he lies, he speaks his native language, for he is a liar and the father of lies.*

Jesus is giving us a lot of information here about Satan and what we can expect to receive if we deal with him. When we cooperate with Satan, knowingly or unknowingly, we are carrying out the desires of Satan. He only cares about himself. He is also at the root of the Spirit of Murder. We see that play out in Genesis with the very first murder by Cain in Genesis out of anger and jealousy, and as a result, Cain used violence to kill his brother.

These behaviors are a result of demonic spirits. Jesus also tells us Satan is not holding to the truth, he cannot because he doesn't have any truth in him so nothing he says will have truth. Jesus calls him a liar, tells us "when he lies" that lies are his native language essentially saying every word he uses to speak is a lie. Jesus concludes with telling us Satan is the father of lies. Lies began with Satan, they are all attributed to Satan and are his main tactic to get what he wants.

Luke 10:16,[6] *"Whoever listens to you listens to me; whoever rejects you rejects me; but whoever rejects me rejects him who sent me."* *The seventy-two returned with joy and said, "Lord, even the demons submit to us in your name." He replied, "I saw Satan fall like lightning from heaven.* (Reference to Isaiah 13*) I have given you authority to trample on snakes and scorpions and to overcome all the power of the enemy; nothing will harm you.*

Jesus is painting a picture of black and white here. Jesus tells us He is the way the truth and the life, He has told us Satan has no truth. So, in verse 16 Jesus is telling us to pick one or the other, we can't have both. If you pick Satan once, that is your choice and that is rejecting Jesus. He references the scripture in Isaiah we talked about where Satan fell from heaven. Then we see who we are in relation to Satan. We have been given the authority to overcome him and when we do, he can't do anything to us. When we don't use our authority - we don't have that assurance.

Matthew 13:18, *"Listen then to what the parable of the sower means: When anyone hears the message about the kingdom and does not understand it, the evil one comes and snatches away what was sown in their heart. This is the seed sown along the path.*

Here Jesus is explaining the parable of the Sower and He starts off with discussing how Satan is there to steal even our opportunity to have a relationship with Him. Do we fall into any of these categories in this parable of having the word being stolen from us? What is our response when hearing the Word? We must guard our hearts and minds in Christ Jesus as we are told in Philippians 4:7.

Jesus also refers to the devil as the evil one. The definition of evil is to be profoundly immoral or wicked. Why do we continually place ourselves in positions to be misled by something profoundly immoral or wicked? We must see through the lies, see through the deceit, help others see through it in love, not bashing each other. We need to decide for ourselves, are we listening to I Am or are we listening to lies. When we find ourselves at a crossroads where we must choose between light and dark, we must seek God. Anything that is not a part of I Am will lead you down a path of lies and destruction. I Am, I Am, I Am is the same yesterday, today and forever.

Chapter 3

We Have Authority Over Demons

It is essential for us to have an understanding of authority before we begin our journey together through this book. We need to know the scriptural basis for the authority Jesus gave us. If we don't have that in place as a foundation, then we shouldn't begin the journey. This foundation begins to lay the groundwork for building confidence to act in faith in our authority. We need to get this understood in our mind, body and spirit to be able to conquer and cancel the plans of the enemy, evicting him from our lives.

Before we start, I want to share something really important about authority. While we are going to discuss our authority by laying the framework and foundation of how we have our authority scripturally, we first need to approach the subject with our hearts. All the reading and scripture in the world will do nothing to convince you if you need to be convinced. As we start this, pray and ask the Lord to reveal it to you in your Spirit. Then you must believe by faith that you have the authority. When we don't believe in faith, we limit our ability to operate with the authority Jesus gave us.

Alright let's get started. The first thing I want to address is a misconception out there among Christians. This misconception functions as an excuse to do nothing, and it is definitely a lie from the enemy. The lie is simple: not

31

everyone has authority. The lie further contends that authority is reserved just for pastors or for a special few. One thing a lack of belief will do is prevent us from moving forward with strength in our authority. Every believer has authority. Whether you feel like you have it, whether you exercise it, whether you understand it - we all have it. It was a gift given to us from Jesus. He had to endure death, hell and the grave in order to gain the victory which gave Him the right to give that authority to us to use in His name. We need to treasure this gift. Remember that Satan does not want us to learn about our authority because he doesn't want us to use it. He will fight us more on this issue than anything else in our lives. If it is that important for Satan to want to keep it from us, we need to be that much more diligent to know about it. Considering the cost Jesus paid on our behalf, enabling us to have the authority, we should be encouraged to want to use His name for our protection and expansion of His Kingdom.

Let's take a look at some scripture. I want to show the progression from God giving it to Jesus and then Jesus giving it to us.

We are going to start in John 3:31. Let me set the scene here. We are with John the Baptist out in the Judean countryside; John is baptizing people with a baptism of repentance. Now remember that John was given the Holy Spirit when he was in the womb, so he already had what was not yet available to anyone at that time, but what we now have available to us as a believer. Anyhow, John is explaining that he is not the Messiah but was sent ahead of the Messiah. Now let's see what he says about Jesus specifically in John 3:31, *"The one who comes from above is above all; the one who is from the earth belongs to the earth, and speaks as one from the earth. The one who comes from heaven is above all. He testifies to what he has seen and heard, but no one accepts his testimony. Whoever has accepted it has certified that God is truthful. For the one whom God has sent speaks the words of God, for God gives the Spirit without limit. The Father loves the Son and has placed everything in his hands. Whoever believes in the Son has eternal life, but whoever rejects the Son will not see life, for God's wrath remains on them."*

I personally think this scripture gets frequently overlooked. There is a question with this scripture as to whether this is a quote from John the Baptist or John the Disciple, the author of this book. It doesn't really matter; the end result is the same in terms of the testimony being given. I happen to believe it is the Holy Spirit in John, testifying to the relationship between God and Jesus and discussing how the Holy Spirit is given without limit. It also tells us God has placed everything in the hands of Jesus. This is an important revelation to those present when John was speaking, and to us as well. This is how God introduces Jesus to the world and reveals this is God's plan for the future. It is God who then personally announces Jesus is His Son when Jesus comes up out of the water after being baptized by John the Baptist. This also reveals to us a transfer of authority to Jesus directly from heaven.

Here are three places where Jesus is telling us the Father has given all authority to Him. Let's start with Matthew 11:27, *"All things have been committed to me by my Father. No one knows the Son except the Father, and no one knows the Father except the Son and those to whom the Son chooses to reveal him.*

Now Matthew again 28:18, *"Then Jesus came to them and said, "All authority in heaven and on earth has been given to me. "*

Here is another Luke 10:22, *"All things have been committed to me by my Father. No one knows who the Son is except the Father, and no one knows who the Father is except the Son and those to whom the Son chooses to reveal him."* Does that sound familiar? It confirms Matthew 11:27.

Here is Paul writing to the Colossians, explaining authority to them. Colossians 2:10, *"and in Christ you have been brought to fullness. He is the head over every power and authority"*

These scriptures give us the foundation we need to know that Jesus has been given control of everything from God. There is no doubting that relationship, nothing is missing - It is everything. The Creator of the Universe, the Great I Am, the one who Was before there "was" anything, or one of my favorite names for him, The Ancient One, put everything in the hands of Jesus. Now let's see what Jesus did with it.

As believers, we know that Jesus took our sins, sacrificed himself on the cross to redeem us for those sins. A lot of Christianity being taught focuses on the cross, and we get stuck there at the foot of the cross. Yes, we do need to come to the cross, nothing happens without that, but Jesus did not remain at the cross, and neither should we. He was resurrected and He ascended to heaven to be with his Father. When He ascended, He left us with gifts. He left us the tools we need to use to accomplish what He asked of us for Him and for the glory of His Father.

Here is Paul again, describing what was done at the cross and where we stand now. Colossians 2:13, *" When you were dead in your sins and in the uncircumcision of your flesh, God made you alive with Christ. He forgave us all our sins, having canceled the charge of our legal indebtedness, which stood against us and condemned us; he has taken it away, nailing it to the cross. And having disarmed the powers and authorities, he made a public spectacle of them, triumphing over them by the cross"*

So yes, the cross made everything possible, but Jesus triumphed over the cross. He didn't stay there. If he had, none of us would have the gift of life He gave to us. He had to overcome death. Paul describes it this way in Ephesians 1:20, *"I pray that the eyes of your heart may be enlightened in order that you may know the hope to which he has called you, the riches of his glorious inheritance in his holy people, and his incomparably great power for us who believe. That power is the same as the mighty strength he exerted when he raised Christ from the dead and seated him at his right hand in the heavenly realms, far above all rule and authority, power and dominion, and every name that is invoked, not only in the present age but also in the one to come. And God placed all things under his feet and appointed him to be head over everything for the church, which is his body, the fullness of him who fills everything in every way."*

Complete Victory, that's what Paul is telling us here, Victory in the name of Jesus!

He goes on to say this in Ephesians 2:4, *"But because of his great love for us, God, who is rich in mercy, made us alive with Christ even when we were dead in transgressions—it is by grace you have been saved. And God raised us up with Christ and seated us with him in the heavenly realms in Christ Jesus, in order that in the coming ages he might show the incomparable riches of his grace, expressed in his kindness to us in Christ Jesus. For it is by grace you have been saved, through faith—and this is not from yourselves, it is the gift of God."* Jesus then ascended to the right hand of God, and God has raised us there with Jesus.

35

Recently I had lunch with a young woman. I am beginning to mentor her, and we are starting with some baseline discussions. I need to understand who she is and where she wants to go with the Lord. The Lord gave me a word of knowledge about her situation, so I knew what she was experiencing started when she was about 3-4 years old. The Lord revealed to me the issue, but I needed to know how that impacted her so we could deal with all of it, not just bits and pieces. It broke my heart when she spoke, her spirit was wounded, you could see it, hear it and feel it. She appeared defeated, but I knew she wasn't. I watched her look down and move her falafel around (we were at a Mediterranean restaurant) and I was to wait to speak. I wanted to tell her she can overcome this, but I'm having to wait until the Holy Spirit tells me I can talk.

As a sidenote, there is baggage we carry around, most of us for years, and it becomes a part of us, shapes our personality and affects our relationships. I would say we generally have more than one piece of baggage we are carrying around. A lot of times, I have found the biggest piece of baggage is the one we started carrying first and then the smaller ones came after as a result.

Ok, back to the story, finally, after she said all the things she needed to say, I understood why I needed to wait. She laid out all the places where demons had been attacking her and confirmed how it affected her generationally. When I was able to reveal to her what the Lord told me, she completely lit up. You could see this belief sprouting, and the deeper we spoke about how the Lord can remove this from her life, the lighter her countenance became. She was more than happy to do the homework she needed to do so we could deal with all of it, not just the bits and pieces. An eviction notice is coming in her life!

Exercising the authority that Jesus gave us isn't some ethereal discussion. This really should be our everyday conversation among believers. This is something we need, something we use, something that defeats the enemy and kills his plans, activities, tactics and allows us to evict him from our lives. This is how move in **Conquering Our Unseen Enemies**. That's what we need, so let's get back to what Jesus has to say about giving us authority in His name.

In *Matthew 10:1 "Jesus called his twelve disciples to him and gave them authority to drive out impure spirits and to heal every disease and sickness."*

In Luke 10:19, Jesus tells us *"I have given you authority to trample on snakes and scorpions and to overcome all the power of the enemy; nothing will harm you."*

Jesus had all the power from God, and He delegated that authority to us to use against Satan. We need to know that Satan coming against us is real. We see it every day in our schools, in our government, regardless of which side you are on, and unfortunately in our churches. Peter tells us in 1 Peter 5:8, *"Be alert and of sober mind. Your enemy the devil prowls around like a roaring lion looking for someone to devour"*

Jesus tells us the same thing in John 10:10, *"the enemy comes to steal, kill and destroy."*

Because Satan's attacks are real, we need to have these conversations out in the open and know our authority. Jesus expects us to use it and to do so without fear.

Mark 16:16 tells us, *"Whoever believes and is baptized will be saved, but whoever does not believe will be condemned. And these signs will accompany those who believe: In my name they will drive out demons; they will speak in new tongues; they will pick up snakes with their hands; and when they drink deadly poison, it will not hurt them at all; they will place their hands on sick people, and they will get well."*

We know from 1 John 4:4, *"You, dear children, are from God and have overcome them, because the one who is in you is greater than the one who is in the world."*

As a result of sin, Adam gave Satan the right to rule this world. Adam didn't give Satan the right to rule over us. I have heard so many times how we are helpless here until Jesus returns. I have even heard someone say that after they've been told the authority is theirs. That attitude and belief is nonsense. You can't help people who don't want to believe. We need to believe and know we are victorious because Jesus is victorious. And 1 Corinthians 6:17 tells us, *"But whoever is united with the Lord is one with him in spirit."* We are seated with Christ.

A few things about authority I want to be clear about.

·   Our authority rests entirely in the name of Jesus, so when we use it, we need to be very clear and say the authority is in the name of Jesus. Leaving Jesus out will result in no change.

·   We only use our authority in places where Jesus would use his authority, for kingdom purposes

·   Our authority is only over Satan and his demons. We cannot wield authority over others, including other households or to control behaviors of someone who does not agree with us. Attempting to use it as manipulation is witchcraft.

· We can stand in the gap for others who are baby Christians and not yet spiritually mature enough to use their authority

· We should not continually stand in the gap or pray for someone not willing to pray for themselves. God expects us to walk, grow and start doing things for ourselves.

· Anyone, believer or non-believer who states the authority believers have in Christ is not real or does not work or is dead is speaking contrary to the Word and ultimately calling God a liar. As a believer, we would simply rebuke that lie from Satan.

· We cannot use our authority to direct angels what to do for our benefit. Angels respond to the Word, and they will not work to meet our needs that are not part of His will. They minister to us, they are not our employees.

· Most importantly, we must always depend on the Holy Spirit to direct us in using our authority. He may give us a word of knowledge or give us a specific action to follow.

Our authority in Jesus complements and supports Spiritual warfare principles, so we will continue to build on our foundation of authority as we continue on our journey together.

Chapter 4

Words Matter in the Kingdoms

Before we get too far down the road on our journey, let's stop a minute and address the most important weapon and weakness we have that produces an immediate and long-term affect in our lives. Most people do not realize our words and how the words we choose to use matter in the outcomes of everything we do.

Our lives don't just exist in the natural realm. We are affected one way or the other by what is happening around us in the spirit realm. We can shift our outcomes by choosing words inspired by the Holy Spirit or words inspired by the enemy. It's our choice.

Let's start off by looking at Proverbs 18:21, *"The tongue has the power of life and death, and those who love it will eat its fruit."* Let's take this a step further with James 3:9-12, *"With the tongue we praise our Lord and Father, and with it we curse human beings, who have been made in God's likeness. Out of the same mouth come praise and cursing. My brothers and sisters, this should not be. Can both fresh water and saltwater flow from the same spring? My brothers and sisters, can a fig tree bear olives, or a grapevine bear figs? Neither can a salt spring produce fresh water."*

What are some of the phrases we say regularly without putting much thought into what we are actually saying?

You're killing me!

41

What a loser!

I can never win!

That boy will never learn!

I'm never going to……get that promotion, be able to afford…., understand….

I'm sick and tired of……

Our words are powerful. Our words carry the authority we have in Jesus. As a result, how we use our words matter. James 3:5 tells us this, *"Likewise, the **tongue** is a small part of the body, but it makes great boasts. Consider what a great forest is set on fire by a small spark."* When we say things in the negative, like I am sick and tired, we are coming into agreement with the one who would happily make us sick and tired. We are stating that is what we are and therefore, don't be surprised when you find yourself in a perpetual state of sickness and fatigue.

If you don't believe words matter, take a look at what Jesus tells us in Matthew 12:36-37, *"But I tell you that everyone will have to give account on the day of judgment for every empty word they have spoken. For by your words you will be acquitted, and by your words you will be condemned."* Personally, I don't want to be condemned so I am conscious of the words I chose to speak over myself and others. I want to make sure when I speak, I speak life. This is not a prosperity conversation, or a visualization technique or a karma discussion or a "release of good energy" topic, those are not biblical. Be careful never to call a Biblical principle anything that is derived from Satan. Karma, "energy" and visualization since those techniques are rooted in false religions.

Why am I even addressing this issue? We need to address this issue not only because what we speak in the natural affects what happens to us in the spirit realm but also because the enemy has the ability to obtain legal rights over us by our poor choice of words. Likewise, when we use our words of life or authority, we can direct ministering angels to work on Kingdom activities. I'm not talking about using angels to meet our whim. Angels respond to the Word of God, so when we pray, using scripture, the Holy Spirit can use us to accomplish many things for the Kingdom of God. When we speak over a situation the way the Lord wants us to speak over a situation, the miraculous can happen. Look for example at Jericho. Joshua led his army for 6 days in silence and on the 7th day when they gave a shout, the walls of the city crumbled. The walls of Jericho had places in it that were as thick as 20 feet and as high as 28 feet. I have felt walls which were similar though not as old. The walls at Jericho are believed to be 8000-9000 BC, and the Mycenean walls in Greece I felt were only about 1300 BC, but they were incredibly solid. So, to have a group of soldiers shout and have the city walls collapse was not done by mere voices; it was a supernatural event occurring the way the Lord advised them. When we use our voices, our words in cooperation with the Lord, anything is possible.

Still not convinced? If we believe in the Bible, then we have to believe in Jericho, and then we have to believe that our words have power. We can't have it any other way, or we are calling the author of the Bible, the Holy Spirit inspired Bible, a liar. If we know all of the above to be true, then we have to know when we speak the opposite of what the Holy Spirit desires, we still have power in our words, we just activate the enemy.

In 2022, my 26-year-old son had a stroke. I want to share with you a detail from the story so if you are in this situation, or one similar, you know how to handle it. We are going to go back to this story a few times in our time together here with different levels of detail or areas of focus because it provides a lot of strong examples for our ongoing conversation.

This particular day was a long one. It started with a surgery where a stint was placed to allow for the blood flow to the left side of his brain. Two of his carotids were no longer pumping blood to his brain. The surgery seemed to be a success, but he was complaining of intense pain all day. They tried multiple options; none was relieving the pain. We weren't allowed to stay with him over night in the hospital, so we stayed past visitor hours to meet the new nurse after the shift change. In that last hour we did notice a change in his behavior. I had never been in that situation before and quite frankly, I was happy he was alive and had been talking to us throughout the day. In the last hour though, he was different. Now, looking back, the image of him as I walked away to leave in the capable hands of the nurse, that image of him is burned in my mind. Why did I walk away, why did I not speak up? I know better than that. Anyhow, we reluctantly left his side. His wife and I were by his side all day, and I was going to take her home after we left. They only lived a mile or so from us at the time. I dropped her off, came home and gave the latest update to my husband. There were still covid restrictions so only two people were allowed in ICU, and they were very restrictive about how many could be in the waiting room. I remember sitting down on the couch, reclining a bit and texting everyone that the surgery was a success. After I sent the last text it was about 8:15, and I watched my hand lay down still holding my phone and just as it touched the arm of the couch, it rang. It was my daughter in law. I answered and she was incredibly upset. The hospital called and stated that my son was going into emergency surgery, and they didn't think he was going to make it.

We jumped in the car and headed back to the hospital. I called all my prayer warriors and the last several people in my call list just because. And then I prayed a prayer that came from a place I had never met inside me before. It was from such a depth in me that my throat was raw by the time we drove the 10 minutes back to the hospital. We were escorted by a security guard to ICU. My daughter in law got there at about the same time, we walked hand in hand to hold each other up and in solidarity that we were going to get through this together. When we turned the corner and entered his room again, we saw him lying there; he looked lifeless, it was very difficult to see. I wasn't prepared mentally to see him that way and neither was his wife. The surgeon was still on his way, everyone else attending to him in ICU was very solemn because they called us so we could say goodbye. The ICU doctor was preparing us for the worst and their word choice over their belief of his outcome was hanging out there in the air.

There are two things you can do in a situation that looks perilous. One is to confront it head on, and the other is to run the other way. It's like fight or flight, but it's the spirit realm, so it does feel differently. In our situation, I saw my son and put the immediate shock aside; there was work to do there. If I need to be emotional, I could do it later. I was not about to let any words of death spoken over my son remain any longer. My daughter in law, got stuck, she couldn't work past the immediate shock, and she began to breakdown. All the stress of the last few days had mounted, and she was struggling. She began to say things that her heart felt, normal - natural things you would say if you were in that situation. It

45

was heart breaking. I knew she didn't have it in her to be strong, and I didn't have the time to be strong for me and for her. As she spoke, she repeated the words she had been told by the doctors and was letting what she saw in the natural overtake her emotions. The words she spoke were not life. We could only use words of life only in that moment. I turned to her, I grabbed her by the face, and I said, "I'm sorry, you know I have to do this." She nodded yes, and I rebuked her and told her why we had to speak words of life. It was enough to wake her up and allow her to refocus and change the direction of her thoughts and words. Then I could move to my son and pray over his life replacing all the words of death spoken over him with words of life.

When something has been spoken over you or someone in your life, and they are not words of life, or words that are Holy Spirit inspired, but rather something you would associate with the enemy, rebuke it. Even if it is your friend, or someone from church say upfront, "I'm sorry, but I rebuke that word of ...." and then speak life. We can't worry about hurt feelings. When Jesus predicted his death and Peter responded that this would never happen, how did Jesus respond? Think about it, Peter just did what many of us do. Someone says something, and we try to quell their spirit and say oh, no, that will never happen. We think we are doing the right thing. What ultimately happened? *"Jesus turned and said to Peter, Get behind me Satan."* Jesus rebuked Peter right to his face then and there. On one hand, we must be bold and rebuke where it is called for in a situation. On the other hand, we need to be mindful of what we say and not say things where we shouldn't that also might interfere.

Let's look at Proverbs 21:23, *"Those who guard their mouths and their **tongues** keep themselves from calamity"* We don't do this today. In the American culture, we take free speech to another level. We use it more as an excuse to attack another, instead of what was intended which was for us to be able to have our own thoughts and not be arrested for saying what we think or believe. It was a good thing once upon a time, but too much of a good thing has turned into chaos with social media. People say the most horrific things through social media that they wouldn't say in person. Some people are so extreme it is not enough to say something in person, they have to back it up with violent acts or with acts of destruction. It's complete chaos, and it is all satanically driven. Take hold and account of what you say. When we add to it, we add to chaos in our lives. Proverbs 12:18 tells it another way, *"The words of the reckless pierce like swords, but the **tongue** of the wise brings healing."*

So, let's look back at the phrases we started off with:

You're killing me!: This seems innocent enough, but you literally are saying something is killing you and under no circumstances would I speak that over myself, as a joke, or for any reason. This statement qualifies as a self-imposed curse. This is not speaking life.

What a loser!: This we usually say after we have experienced something negative involving another person or just to be mean. Even if you truly believe there is some truth to it, you don't need to say that and speak that over someone's life. We don't want to have to account for it later or be a part of something that does result from words we have chosen to say over someone else. This is not speaking life.

I can never win!: Again, why would I want to say that over myself. Another example of a self-imposed curse. This is not speaking life.

That boy will never learn!: This is similar to the loser comment, but more definitive. To use never and say something will never happen is you being willing to curse someone else. It becomes a self-fulfilling prophecy. This is not speaking life.

I'm never going to......get that promotion, be able to afford...., understand....: Another example of a self-imposed curse. This is not life.

I'm sick and tired of......: Self-imposed curse again. These are not life words.

Words matter. Things we say seem innocent enough at the time, but they can have repercussions. We need to make sure what we say matters for us in the best possible way. In the way that Jesus would speak over us, by speaking life in agreement with God's Kingdom.

Part 2:

Dark Forces in Motion

Chapter 5

Misconceptions on Demonic Topics

I want to address some common questions that will also serve to clarify some misconceptions. It's important to address those first before we start talking about how demons work so we are all on the same page from the get-go. The amount of bad information out there is overwhelming, and if you are trying to learn, a lot of what is out is conflicting. Let's start from the basics and keep it simple. The misconceptions we will be discussing are: What is a Demon? What is a Believer? Can believers be demon possessed? Is casting out demons real and can we really cast out (evict) demons the way Jesus did? What authority do we have to tell evicted demons where to go? Can we evict demons in non-believers?

Alright, let's get started and kick it off with:

What is a demon?

A demon is a spirit, a person without a body, otherwise called disembodied. Generally speaking, we cannot see demons, but they can choose to make themselves visible as both darkness and disguise themselves as an angel of light. There are instances where they can be seen by individuals who have been given the gift to see into the spirit realm; the term often used for someone who can see in the spirit realm is a Seer, but at times the Holy Spirit will allow you to see a demon spirit if necessary. Demons are in Satan's hierarchy and have roles and ranks. Demons need a place to indwell, and they prefer humans, but will take an animal. An example of this is in Matthew 8:29 when Jesus casts out the demons from the two demon possessed men and permits the demons to enter a herd of pigs. When a demon indwells in a person, it considers that person to be its "house". Jesus gives us a picture of this in Matthew 12:43-44, *"when an impure spirit comes out of a person, it goes through arid and dry places seeking rest and does not find it. Then it says, I will return to the **House** I left"*. A demon is a spiritual enemy of all believers, but also of humanity in general. Their ultimate objective is to keep people from knowing Jesus as their savior. If you already are a believer, then they want to keep you from knowing your authority and being effective. The way they achieve their objective is through tempting, deceiving, accusing, condemning, pressuring, defiling, resisting, opposing, controlling, stealing, afflicting, killing, and destroying. Jesus told us in John 10:10, *"the thief comes only to steal, kill and destroy."* Mark 9:17, gives us an example of a man who brings his son to Jesus because a demon has taken away the child's ability to speak. Luke 4:33, gives us another example demonic activity of a man who was possessed by an impure spirit, and the demons began to cry out at the sight of Jesus, *"Go away! What do you want with us, Jesus of Nazareth? Have you come to destroy us? I know who you are- the Holy One of God!"* That same event is given to us in Mark 1:23. Mark 5:2 gives us a picture of a demon possessed man who was incredibly violent and would not only harm others, but would cut himself, something we see today as well. Demons have characteristics that identify their role in the Kingdom of Satan. The characteristic also identifies their name. For example, someone who has addiction issues may have an indwelling of a demon named Addiction. Demonic names correspond to their role, or their job. We will break down these demon names more we discuss demon groupings and even further when we look at specific demon groupings.

We need to clarify at this point one thing when I refer to a believer. What I am specifically saying in reference to a believer is someone who has accepted Jesus as their Savior. Someone who believes that Jesus is the Son of God, who died for their sins, was resurrected, and ascended back into heaven to the right hand of God. A believer is someone who has repented of their sins and is faithful and committed to serve Jesus. I don't particularly like to use the term Christian because many religious groups refer to themselves as Christians but are not believers. For what we are discussing on this journey together, the distinction is necessary and requires clarification. Our authority comes from Jesus so someone who is a Christian but not a believer in Jesus will not have the authority. We discussed that in Part 1, but the scriptural reference for that is Mark 16:17. which states…*in my name they will drive out demons."* Luke 9:1, reveals *"when Jesus has called the Twelve together, he gave them power and authority to drive out all demons"* and Matthew 10:1 where Jesus gave his *authority to drive out impure spirits.*

Ok, let's move onto the next question. Can believers be demon possessed?

Most people will answer this question no, which is correct. Once we belong to Christ, we cannot be possessed by Satan as we belong to Jesus. Satan does not have the legal right to "possess" a believer any more than I have the legal right to tell my neighbor they cannot drive their own car. What isn't well understood or accepted is that believers can be demonized. So, if I stood around my neighbors' car, preventing them from using it even though I don't own it, I am certainly interfering with their use of the car. Likewise, believers can have demons indwell to demonize them and not realize that is what is happening. Again, Matthew 12:43 addresses the fact that demons indwell in a person. Once we get to a mindset where we don't defend our "house," we are allowing the demons to work unchallenged against us. I would say if you asked anyone sitting in church today if they have any demons needed cast out, after you got past the looks of insult, you would hear a resounding "NO!" In reality, the answer should be, "Yes, please and thank you!" We all have at one time or another demons working against us, demonizing us. Sometimes over little nit picky things and sometimes over big sins we are carrying in our lives. It's not something to be embarrassed about, it's reality. If we look at the delivery ministry of Jesus, he didn't just cast out demons for "those people"- the ones we shun in public. He addressed demons in the lives of everyday people. For years I used to wonder why Jesus had such an active deliverance ministry, and yet we don't see active deliverance ministries like that today. Were demons more prevalent in ancient days? The truth is we have the same demons today as when Jesus walked the earth, but today we are more willing to embrace them, hide behind them or not bother to address them at all. There are people active in deliverance ministry, but we are more likely to cast the deliverance minister out of our lives than the demons.

At some point you may hear me use the word evict instead of cast out. I prefer evict because it is a better definition of what needs to happen. To evict someone is to force them to leave a place, which is supported by law. In English, cast out is more to exclude someone from a group or place. We need to go into it with the idea of forcing those demons out with the message, "and don't come back!"

Moving onto the next question. Is casting out demons real and can we really cast out (evict) demons the way Jesus did?

Casting out, or evicting demons is very real but generally not as crazy and dramatic as the movies make it out to be. The Holy Spirit is always in control, so you need to make sure you are yielding to the Holy Spirit. Speaking to whether we too can evict the same way Jesus did, we refer back to Matthew 10:1, where Jesus gave His *authority to drive out impure spirits*, and Mark 16:17, which states…*in my name they will drive out demons..*" We have the authority and the responsibility to evict these demons in the name of Jesus. Paul gives us a really good example in Acts 16:16, when he is on one of his missionary journeys and is staying in Philippi. He was being followed around by a woman who practiced divination. She followed him for a time before the Holy Spirit directed him to say, "*I command you in the name of Jesus Christ to depart from her!*" This led to the beginning of several problems for Paul and Silas, which is not our focus, but understand that Paul's actions took incredible faith and courage. We can be just as effective as Jesus was and, in some ways, more so because he was only with us for a short time. If you are interested in learning more about the history behind this type of demon Paul evicted, I did a video on this on my YouTube Channel, Life Journey with Dawn Simmons where I visited Delphi, Greece and share that visit and explain what Paul was addressing. It's titled *"How Delphi shaped the history of the world."*

Next question, what authority do we have to tell evicted demons where to go?

The short answer to this is very little. Let me explain what the Bible reveals to us about this issue. There is a set time and place for when demons are sent to be tormented. Only God knows the set time. In Matthew 8 we see several instances of Jesus evicting demons and healing people. This chapter is full of His miracles, He also calms the storm here; it's just a magnificent chapter. Let's look closer at 8:29 where Jesus encounters two demon possessed men who were out casts from their community, living in tombs - so they were set apart already in the natural. In this particular case the demons caused these men to be violent. Starting with verse 28, *"When he (Jesus) arrived at the other side of the region of the Gadarenes, two demon possessed men coming from the tombs met him. They were so violent that no one could pass that way. "What do you want with us, Son of God?" they shouted.* (these demons recognized Jesus) *"Have you come here to torture us before the appointed time?"* The Book of Revelation explains what that appointed time will be like, but from this we see that there is an appointed time at which these demons will no longer be allowed to torment you and me. Let's go back now and look at how Jesus responds, *some distance from them a large herd of pigs was feeding. The demons begged Jesus, "If you drive us out, send us into the herd of pigs." He said "Go!" so they came out and went into the pigs, and the whole herd rushed down the steep bank into the lake and died in the water".* This story used to puzzle me. These poor innocent pigs were living their life, doing what pigs were supposed to be doing and then...bam...they are dead, a pretty violent death in my opinion. As an animal lover, I'd get stuck on that point and miss the other points that are revealed here. First, we see Jesus took care of these two men and evicted the demons. Presumably these two men were Gentiles by the way which was unusual for Jesus or the disciples to minister to Gentiles at that time. Second, the demons tried to talk and stall the inevitable. Third, the demons tried to negotiate, and Jesus let them negotiate. Fourth, when the demons left, they transferred themselves to pigs because pigs are better than nothing. The demons claimed not allowing them to make that transfer qualified as premature torment for them. Fifth, a herd of pigs, these men had several demons indwelling, not one or two, but a herdful. The same account in Mark actually reveals the number of demons was 2000. Sixth, Jesus surely knew the end result with the pigs. Seventh, even the pigs did not want these demons, they were scared and chose this end rather than a life with these demons. Animals sense demons better than we do. Whether logic was applied, I have no idea, but something made these pigs run, a natural reaction to a huge group of demons running at you. Eighth, demons were permitted to go into the pigs for the benefit of the men being tormented. Lastly, demons are unclean. Jesus confirmed that to us by allowing them to transfer to these pigs, considered unclean animals by the Jewish law, practiced at that time.

So now back to that original question. We cannot in our authority send demons to hell. We can command them to leave, but unless the Holy Spirit tells you something specific to say at that time, we cannot tell them where they should go. I have only had one occasion, for a deliverance where the Holy Spirit directed me to tell the demons to go someplace specific when they were evicted. In my experience, it's just not common for us to have authority to tell them where to go. There are many people out there who say otherwise, but I am basing my answer to this question on what the Bible says and what Jesus revealed to us. An answer based on anything else is nonsense and should be dismissed.

Ok, we are on our last question now. Can we evict demons in non-believers?

The answer here is technically yes, but let me explain how that would have to happen. We touched on this earlier, but the issue comes down to legal rights. When we accept Jesus as our Savior and become a member of the Kingdom of God, we belong to Jesus. Legally, Satan cannot stay to indwell in us if we use our authority and command him to leave. We are then responsible to keep our "house" clean. In a situation where the person requesting the demons be evicted is not a believer, the eviction must be done by someone who does have that authority, a believer. As long as the non-believer explicitly states they want the demon gone, then the demon has to leave once directed to do so. The question really becomes one of whether it should be done. Someone who has not accepted Jesus does not have access to the legal right of protection from Jesus. If that non-believer is not then equipped with authority to keep demons out once they are on their own, a day later, a week later or a year later, then what happens? Setting someone up for a Matthew 12:44 scenario is not what we should be doing. The better approach is to lead that person to the saving grace of Jesus first and then address the demons being evicted. Just don't forget a new believer will need support until they can stand on their own. Not many new believers will know how to fight off demons; they are still learning what the Bible is and may not know much about the Holy Spirit. So that is a deliverance that should be proceeded with in caution.

Well, now we have the beginnings of a foundation in understanding dark forces in motion. Let's keep going and see how they work together.

Chapter 6

What are Demon Groupings?

It is time to lay some groundwork for understanding demon groupings and how demon groupings can form. I will also share with you some of my experiences in working with people to deliver them from the bondage of demons.

In the previous chapter, we talked about a demon being a spirit, a person without a body, otherwise called disembodied. We discussed demons are in Satan's hierarchy and have roles and ranks. As well as explaining demons need a place to indwell and they prefer humans but will take an animal. We saw an example of this in Matthew 8:29 when Jesus casts out the demons from the two demon possessed men and permits the demons to enter a herd of pigs. That example is also discussed in Mark, and we find out that the leader of those demons referred to himself as Legion because the number of demons was 2000. In that parable, Jesus gave us a remarkable example of a demon grouping that He was able to cast out all 2000 at one time. In my experience, it doesn't always work that way. I appreciate that we do have that Biblical example available to us so that we know what we face will generally be easier to manage. The reason I say that is because as we also discussed in Chapter 2, demons, like Satan, will have characteristics that identify their role in the Kingdom of Satan. The characteristic also identifies their name. In reality, this makes it far easier on us to deal with than if say these demons were named Bob, Mary and

59

Jennifer. With those names I don't know anything about what I am dealing with and quite frankly the less I have to actually deal with the demon directly the better. By having them be named by their role or we could even say by their specialized responsibility, because once a demon indwells, they must perform their responsibility. With that knowledge, we can quickly get to the heart of an issue and know why we are dealing with a particular demon. This will ensure we are addressing the root of the issue. Once we get to the root of the issue, then we know we are likely dealing with the strongman.

Let's break all that down a bit so we can walk through a demon grouping from the beginning and see how demon groupings form. I want to be clear about demon roles. Demons function as experts, specialists, in a particular area for example: anxiety. Their entire purpose is to create anxiety in you at any opportunity, and if there aren't enough opportunities then they will help to create an opportunity. The way a demon of anxiety functions may be through several different processes, but they will find multiple ways to get their end result. Their process will change depending on the person, the place, the circumstances, and external factors. Demons know the person they are demonizing very well. Do not assume that you are being demonized one day just out of the blue. Do not assume that one day you are being demonized, and the next day you are not. Their sole purpose is to work you into the worst possible state they can possibly achieve to ultimately have control and domination over you. The entire objective of Satan is domination. To dominate each of us, to ultimately dominate this world, and then to overthrow the Lord and dominate God is his goal and always has been. They plan to achieve their goal one person at a time if that is what it takes. If we talk, act, think or do anything with any other perspective than Satan is there to dominate us - then we are lying to ourselves and positioning ourselves to be dominated without the ability to put up much of a fight. Denial of demons and their purpose is the beginning of a loss. This is not conspiracy theory discussion. This is truth. Hosea 4:6 says that we are destroyed for our lack of knowledge. Jesus is very clear in John 10:10 when He tells us, "*the enemy came to steal, kill and destroy...*" If nothing else I say in our time here today resonates with you, at least take away this one point. The enemy is real, and he exists to dominate and destroy you. This is not a game, this is not my trying to scare you, this is reality. Ok, that is more than one point but nonetheless, I need you to understand the severity of the condition - the enemy is working to get you into their negative domain every single day.

I stated before that the demon knows the person they are demonizing well. I want to explain something about that. Let's use an analogy. Have any of you ever gotten a call from the best restaurant in your country advising that the chef is out sick, and they need you to come in and cover him for the night? More than likely, unless we have a world class chef reading here right now, the answer is probably no. Why is that? Well, I can do a few good things in the kitchen that my husband enjoys but if I want to make a good beef wellington, I'm probably going to pull up a Gordon Ramsay recipe to follow along. I took cooking classes from Damiano Carrara, he used to be on Food Network; he and his brother have Carrara's. He's Italian, so if I wanted to make Italian pastries, I'd refer to those recipes he gave me. No way could I show up at a restaurant, put on an apron and start yelling at the sous chefs to speak up or asking how long for the risotto. Right, it just wouldn't happen that way. To get that call I would have needed to prepare for that assignment for a while. Similarly, a demon takes time to get to know the person they demonize. They need to know weaknesses, relationships, how to manipulate us and to deceive us into making poor choices. So how do they do this so well?

Generally speaking, if we use this demon, anxiety as an example; anxiety isn't working alone. Once we open a door that allows the demon legal access to us, then the demon of anxiety will come and indwell. Anxiety typically will then become the strongman, not always, but usually the first one in, is the one to set up shop so to speak and create opportunities for us to allow other legal access through our sins or words. Most frequently, I see where others were allowed in because of words spoken, as we discussed in Chapter 4; so we need to choose our words wisely.

Let's get back to our example, so anxiety comes in and begins to bring in others that are tied to anxiety like fear. As they create opportunities for others to enter, and we oblige because we are caught up in their deception and lies, then the group begins to form. You can think of it like a chain. They join together and create a demonic chain of influence that over time will get bigger and stronger and pretty soon has us in a bondage. These groupings can also be called colonies, clans or families. A particular grouping will form and will control a particular area of a person's life. Let's look back at the example Jesus gave us, and examine this demon called Legion. How do you think he got his name? His name doesn't sound like a characteristic as we have discussed, so why Legion? A grouping covers a particular area. Do you know anyone with "baggage" that affects only one area of their lives? I don't. So, you may have a grouping formed from anxiety, but this person may also have issues or "baggage" because of rejection. Rejection can come in and bring along their demon associates, and now we have two groupings in one person. When we have the strongman called Legion responding to Jesus, his role is to oversee the 2000 demons, how they function and control, or ruin everything in this man's life. The chances are very slim that someone is being demonized by only one demon. They work best together and in particular combinations. So, with anxiety you frequently will see the demons of fear, worry, apprehension. These are frequent but never assume it's always the same. I didn't really enjoy statistics, but I can tell you that the number of demon combinations possible are closer to infinite. Only once have I met someone with several hundred demons - so many we were unable to count them on their way out.

Let's talk a little more about the strongman. Jesus introduces the strongman to us in Matthew 12:29, *"Or again, how can anyone enter a strong man's house and carry off his possessions unless he first ties up the strong man? Then he can plunder his house."* As I said, usually the strongman is the first one to indwell. A strongman is essentially the ruler of the groupings. In a situation where the demons become challenged, you may only hear from the strongman, and the others in the group will simply hide behind the strongman and remain silent. The strategy is that if they hide behind the strongman and you don't know they are present, you will miss their presence, and they can remain even if others are evicted. The opposite can also be the case where maybe you know the name of a lesser demon, but you don't know the strongman. The lesser demon may be evicted, but if the strongman remains, the lesser demon will be better positioned to come back at a later date. Those are the instances where they could return with even more demons in tow. We read that in Matthew 12:43-4,

" *When an impure spirit comes out of a person, it goes through arid places seeking rest and does not find it. Then it says, 'I will return to the house I left.' When it arrives, it finds the house unoccupied, swept clean and put in order. Then it goes and takes with it seven other spirits more wicked than itself, and they go in and live there. And the final condition of that person is worse than the first. That is how it will be with this wicked generation.*"

In relation to deliverance, I want to share a bit about groupings and what I have seen. From my experience there is a strongman, but it will usually take some digging to identify who it is. The reason for that, again, from my experience so it may not be this way for everyone, is that the strongman can be difficult to identify because it has been there so long. Most of the time the strongman is able to enter during childhood when we are the most vulnerable and often times are not protected. From the time of our childhood to adulthood, others may have since joined and that childhood demon is somewhat suppressed. It becomes suppressed because we push it back and try to forget about it or because the demon itself can function just fine in the background with the others in the foreground. Like an orchestra. It's almost like they can function as a puppet master with us as the puppet. Now not everything we do or that happens to us is demonic. Sometimes we are just making bad choices, so do not misunderstand what I am saying. We are ultimately responsible for our decisions, demon influenced or not, because we are also responsible for cleaning out our "house". There would be very few exceptions to this. Someone's mental incapacity or young children who cannot exercise consent would not be held accountable and would create an exception. They would fall under the grace and mercy of a loving God.

About two years ago I was working with a woman, and I was trying to identify the demons that were influencing her. She was willing to admit to some, but not to all that she was aware she had been dealing with. The Holy Spirit revealed to me two of the demons that she did not reveal. Her unwillingness to address all the demons was part of the issue. There were multiple groupings and one of the things I noticed that I want to share with you is that you can have multiple groupings and, in each grouping, there can be duplicates. For example, she had the demon of fear in multiple groups. That fear had managed to work its way through so many areas of her life, it became a part of who she was. She both acknowledged it and accepted it. When you get to that place where you know it and allow it to stay and permeate your existence, it prevents you from moving forward. It prevents you in those areas of your life in which you want to move forward and as a result, you have allowed the enemy to dominate you. In those situations, I cannot help the person; I could not help her. She would not let go of the demons. We must want to evict and be willing to evict.

I have another woman I was working with who was able to identify the specific demons she was dealing with. She also had a demon of fear, but she knew what she had been living with for so many years and was willing to address her demons head on and evict them. There were several issues to address, and the strongman maintained a hold on her to the very end. In her case, she had one strongman and the demons, there were about twenty, and they formed what appeared to me to be more of a web around her heart and her mind. When you have something like that, it can be difficult to hear and to understand the truth. They are specifically trying to blind you, so you are not able to evict them.

Let me give you some examples of groupings so you can understand how they can operate against you and hopefully you can begin to identify them all when you encounter a situation, whether for yourself or someone else. The truth is, it's not something to be ashamed of or embarrassed by; we all deal with this. The number of demons isn't really an indication of anything in and of itself. If someone thinks they only have one demon, they are not being honest with themselves. On average, it is not uncommon for demons count to be in the twenty or even thirty range because they are so specialized. They gain strength in numbers, so it is to their benefit to join forces.

So here are some examples of common demon groupings:

Pride: ego, vanity, self-righteousness, haughtiness, Importance, Arrogance

Guilt: Condemnation, Shame, Unworthiness, Embarrassment

Control: Possessiveness, Dominance, Witchcraft

Depression: Despair, Suicide, Hopelessness, Defeatism, Discouragement, Insomnia

Paranoia: Jealousy, Envy, Suspicion, Distrust, Persecution, Fears, Confrontation

Indecision: Procrastination, Compromise, Confusion, Forgetfulness, Indifference

I tried to choose different types of issues to show how they can link together and create that web effect to dominate multiple areas of our lives. The more you know about groupings and how they work against you, the easier it will be for you to identify them and position yourself to evict them. This is just a small sampling. There are over fifty groupings that I use when identifying demons and the strong man. Even just looking at this list, you can see how Depression can be the strongman. Depression is specific, yet all of these others: despair, suicide, hopelessness, defeatism, discouragement and insomnia can create their own web within the strongman. When they feed off of each other the demons can take you to a place where you don't see a way out. I will tell you the last time I helped someone evict their demons, I gave them some time afterwards to be alone. When I came back, the woman told me how clear her mind was without all the voices. That was awesome. She had been living with that for years, hiding it, and now she was free.

We can all be free, and we can stay free.

Chapter 7

Satan is a Counterfeit to the Holy Spirit

Many Christians don't realize that there are counterfeits to the Holy Spirit. Just today I read about a pastor in Colorado who is accused of several crimes relating to a crypto scheme and pocketing almost half of the proceeds to fund a remodel and a lot of luxury in his life. He says that the Lord told him to do it. Now, if and this is a big if, we give this guy the benefit of the doubt and let's say he did hear a spiritual being leading him to do this - do you think it was really the Holy Spirit or a counterfeit? Counterfeits to the Holy Spirit are common. We are going to discuss this in a broad sense because there are so many elements, but you will have a strong understanding of how Satan counterfeits and leads believers astray if they are not able to discern Truth from Lies.

To start off, let's examine what a counterfeit is - what is the definition? A counterfeit is something made in exact imitation of something valuable or important with the intention to deceive or defraud.

I would say the Holy Spirit is something valuable and important to us as believers. Anything that has an intent to deceive or defraud is not the Truth and therefore a lie, and Jesus tells us Satan is the Father of lies. We talked about that in Chapter 2, and it can be found in John 8:44.

The number of ways Satan counterfeits the Holy Spirit is seemingly endless because the way the Holy Spirit works in our lives is endless. What Satan cannot do, however, is offer us anything truthful, anything fulfilling, anything to live for because he himself has none of those things. How can he offer what he does not have. Jesus on the other hand has all of those things and more, but if we don't truly know Him and have a relationship with Him, Satan can lead us to a place where we begin to have mixed motivations and compromise our values.

Satan's goal is to counterfeit the Truth so it can be watered down and twisted. The more often this is done, the less we notice and our whole foundation in Jesus erodes. We will sing worship songs that have no worship and quote scripture that's not actual scripture in ignorance because Truth is absent.

Paul was continually dealing with counterfeits in his ministry. Here is what he says to the Romans, this is in Romans 1:18-27

Warnings Against Denying the Son

Dear children, this is the last hour; and as you have heard that the antichrist is coming, even now many antichrists have come. This is how we know it is the last hour. They went out from us, but they did not really belong to us. For if they had belonged to us, they would have remained with us; but their going showed that none of them belonged to us.

Let's talk about this for a minute, everyone today is talking about the end of the world and the antichrist, but Paul is using the term to identify the demonic influence that is

70

present with these men. A Spirit of Antichrist originates within the body of Christ. Christ must have a place first for the antichrist to have an existence.

But you have an anointing from the Holy One, and all of you know the truth. I do not write to you because you do not know the truth, but because you do know it and because no lie comes from the truth. Who is the liar? It is whoever denies that Jesus is the Christ. Such a person is the antichrist—denying the Father and the Son. No one who denies the Son has the Father; whoever acknowledges the Son has the Father also.

We know Satan is the father of lies. Satan knows the Truth that Jesus is the Messiah, but seeks to lead you astray and separate you from your relationship with Jesus. This is very common in the church today, and it is how the Muslim religion has been able to become the fastest growing religion.

As for you, see that what you have heard from the beginning remains in you. If it does, you also will remain in the Son and in the Father. And this is what he promised us—eternal life.

I am writing these things to you about those who are trying to lead you astray. As for you, the anointing you received from him remains in you, and you do not need anyone to teach you. But as his anointing teaches you about all things and as that anointing is real, not counterfeit—just as it has taught you, remain in him.

Paul acknowledges that at that time, he was dealing with counterfeits within the church. These counterfeits were leading early Christians astray, exactly as it is happening today. It is happening in our pulpits by leaders who are teaching a false doctrine. Well get into that in a little bit.

71

Let's look at 2 Corinthians 11: 1-15, and see what Paul has to say about what was happening in first century Corinth.

Paul and the False Apostles

I hope you will put up with me in a little foolishness. Yes, please put up with me! I am jealous for you with a godly jealousy. I promised you to one husband, to Christ, so that I might present you as a pure virgin to him. But I am afraid that just as Eve was deceived by the serpent's cunning, your minds may somehow be led astray from your sincere and pure devotion to Christ. For if someone comes to you and preaches a Jesus other than the Jesus we preached, or if you receive a different spirit from the Spirit you received, or a different gospel from the one you accepted, you put up with it easily enough.

Paul is telling them that they are not correctly discerning the Holy Spirit nor that which they know to be the truth. They are accepting that which is coming from Satan with lies to deceive them with a false doctrine and a spirit other than the Holy Spirit.

Verse 5, *I do not think I am in the least inferior to those "super-apostles."*

Paul was using this term; super apostle sarcastically and then goes on to show the dichotomy between himself as a humble servant and his message and what these Judaizers were offering as a "better brand" of Christianity than the truth of the gospel Paul taught them.

I may indeed be untrained as a speaker, but I do have knowledge. We have made this perfectly clear to you in every way. Was it a sin for me to lower myself in order to elevate you by preaching the gospel of God to you free of charge? I robbed other churches by receiving support from them so as to serve you. And when I was with you and needed something, I was not a burden to anyone, for the brothers who came from Macedonia supplied what I needed. I have kept myself from being a burden to you in any way, and will continue to do so. As surely as the truth of Christ is in me, nobody in the regions of Achaia will stop this boasting of mine. Why? Because I do not love you? God knows I do! And I will keep on doing what I am doing in order to cut the ground from under those who want an opportunity to be considered equal with us in the things they boast about. For such people are false apostles, deceitful workers, masquerading as apostles of Christ. And no wonder, for Satan himself masquerades as an angel of light. It is not surprising, then, if his servants also masquerade as servants of righteousness. Their end will be what their actions deserve.

Paul is talking about the judgment that will take place against these men for their antichrist behavior. This antichrist behavior is a part of our culture today which can be found among believers as well. When we begin to evaluate churches for their amenities and not the message, we have a problem. When we are more concerned with wanting people to see us versus how we want God to see us, we have a problem. When we are more focused on self-love vs God's love, we have a problem.

I hear Paul talking about these "super apostles" and when I consider his list of behaviors to what our world is like today, I would compare it to these mega churches we have. If it is a mega church that is truly preaching the Word and the message of salvation through the sacrifice Jesus made for each of us, then that is not a super apostle. It's when we have the Joel Osteen type of preachers, sorry of you are a fan, but the Joel Osteen's of the world are robbing Christianity of the truth of Jesus Christ and of the Holy Spirit. Participating in such a church is participating in culture - not relationship and that is the spirit of the antichrist moving in the church today. Joel's father, John Osteen, was not like that, but unfortunately Joel does not preach a Bible-based message but rather a cultural feel-good message that is a counterfeit to what Jesus told us when He walked this earth. It is our responsibility as believers to discern truth from lies. We will be held accountable for what we believe, what we say, how we influence others and for the way we lived our lives for the kingdom or not.

I heard a statistic the other day. An anonymous survey was done, but it was only done with pastors. Now I am not out to bash pastors. I give you this survey fact to make sure you are aware and are being led by a Bible-based pastor or you will be accountable one day. The survey was pretty long, but one of the questions was:

How much time do you spend every day in prayer?

Do you want to take a guess at the answer? I'll tell you…it was three minutes. Yes, three minutes.

Look, if you want to make sure you are not putting yourself in a position to follow a counterfeit to the Holy Spirit, you need to be able to discern the Holy Spirit from Satan. We all need to be able to open our Bible and read it for ourselves, consistently to develop that discernment. We should be praying and developing our relationship with the Lord to help us with discernment. Likewise, we should make sure we are being led by a pastor who has that same desire to pray and develop their own relationship with the Lord. No one is above being influenced by Satan. We need to know Jesus so well that we could never mistake one for the other.

Chapter 8

Satan is creating "Deniers" in Christianity

I want to share with you a little about the "Deniers" among us in the Christian circles. This is a word the Lord gave me one day during Easter Week, or Resurrection Week, so I will share a few things about that why we are on this subject. First, let's get on to the topic of "Deniers". What is the Lord talking about? When He gave me that word, I have to admit, "Deniers" is not even a word I use so I wrote it down and immediately looked at it, like that word doesn't look right. Is it misspelled? It's just a weird word, and I felt like it broke some rule of grammar that I didn't know, but once I got past my right brained thinking I looked at it again for the heart of what He was telling me. He was asking me to take some time and open my eyes a bit to see the "Deniers" who are denying Him and denying what He did for us. Those who deny the Truth of who He is and of what He did here on earth. "Deniers" are those who deny the truth of the gospel. Now those folks are everywhere; truly they are not hard to spot. What He was asking me to do, however, was specifically to listen to the "Deniers" in the body of Christ. Now "listening" isn't about judgment - it's about understanding where we stand in our belief of the depth of where He stood, where He hung, where He laid and where He rose and walked again.

I'm going to share with you some words I wrote down the day He spoke to me. My original plan was to pay attention over a period of days, but what I am going to share was actually done within an hour. I'll also share a conversation I had, and we'll a share bit about how to handle these types of words when you are in the middle of this kind of situation. It may not happen often for you, but I want you to be equipped when and if it does, because make no mistake about it, it is the Spirit of the Antichrist talking among the body of Christ. The reason we need to talk about this address it is found in Matthew 7:21, where Jesus tells us this: *Not everyone who says to me "Lord, Lord," will enter the kingdom of heaven, but only the one who does the will of my Father who is in heaven. Many will say to Me on that day, "Lord, Lord, did we not prophesy in your name and in your name drive out demons and in your name perform many miracles?" Then I will tell them plainly, "I never knew you. Away from me, you evildoers!"* Here Jesus is telling us the reality of what is going to happen when that time comes and when He sifts; I don't plan to be chaff. I am wheat, and I want you to be wheat too.

So, we are going to go over seven things that were said immediately after the Lord told me to go and listen. Again, these were the words I heard coming from "Christians."

1. "Angels don't communicate with us today or appear to us today; we can no longer see them"

Well, this isn't true because I have seen them, and I am sure many of you have seen them. There are thousands of stories of people, credible people, who have had encounters with angels. While this may not seem harmful, at the root of this comment is the prevalent belief that when the Bible was finished, so were all the supernatural happenings in the world. As if, because we have the Bible, there is no need for the Angels to do anything. We cannot allow this errant

76

thinking into our minds deny what we read in the Book of Revelation. So again, Satan is trying to make us think that the Kingdom of God is done, there is no movement today and that is a lie - also called a denial of Truth.

2.   Demons are not involved in situations where mental health or health issues are present.

This was said by a woman and, unfortunately, I didn't write down my exact response. It occurred about an hour before the Lord gave me my direction so I didn't think to write it down, but I can tell you that I told her something along the lines of - Jesus gave us specific examples where He cast out demons from people who had mental health issues and health issues. If Jesus says the reason for it was demons, then demons are involved in mental health and health issues. We cannot sit here today and say otherwise, that would be denying what Jesus did as documented here and as written countless times in the Bible. To do so is to call Jesus a liar, and I will not allow that nor ever participate in that. If we hear someone say that and tacitly allow it, without speaking up then we are in essence, agreeing with it. We are not trying to argue, but we must speak the truth in such a situation. We are the Truth in His name.

3.   The Bible has been edited, books have been left out, men have edited it

Now this statement is actually true, but what is being implied for the reasons being stated is a lie and a denial of Truth. The Bible is edited. Most people don't realize that there was set criteria used to determine which books were included in the Bible. One of the issues that persists today is confusion over what should or shouldn't be included in the Bible. We know the Bible is God Breathed to those who wrote it and for some, the very fact that there are books that were previously included or excluded angers them, and so they don't want to believe any of it. That is pure nonsense and an excuse to avoid being accountable and living in sin. The people who seem to get the most upset by it and use it to justify turning their back on Christianity and don't know anything about the part of the Bible that is included. The criteria used was based on a number of things, but a few of the relevant things that matter include taking into consideration the established beliefs of first century Christians and what was accepted by them as true. The reason for that criteria is because the first century Christians were there in the beginning when Paul and the Apostles and Jesus were among them and able to guide them and teach them. They were firsthand witnesses, and their testimony is reliable and credible. The date was also important. To be included in the Bible, the book had to be written within a time period while the church was being established. You would not include something from the second century in the Bible because the first century Christians would not have included it in their teachings. Another thing to be considered was the author. Even if the author was first century, if what was written was heard from a guy, who heard it from a guy, who heard it from a guy - it didn't get in the Bible. You had to have a relationship that could be verified by those who were the original teachers of Christianity. So tangential authors were excluded. The rationale was to not include any teachings that were not known to be included in the original church teachings. Are there some in there that should be? Yes, we know there are some letters of Paul's that were lost because he mentions it, but if the Lord allowed them to be lost, then He must not have needed it and whatever was addressed must be covered elsewhere for us.

4.   Claiming to be a Christian but also claiming not to know Jesus because He is not God, there are other ways to God.

This one came up a lot. I am sure you hear that as well. There is only one way to God. We can't skirt around that. We aren't trying to argue with anyone, but we should know why we believe, what we believe, and be able to quote the scripture. The easiest one to use as our support is in John 14:6. "Jesus answered, I am the way, the truth and the life. No one comes to the Father except through me." Anyone saying otherwise is speaking a lie which is a denial of Truth.

5.   I don't believe people go to hell. If everyone is loved, then it doesn't matter. Hell is just a scary story

This garbage statement hits on two lies. The first lie: if everyone is loved, then it doesn't matter. Well, God is love, yes, but He is also Holy, and God will not love that which is evil. We have free choice and people use that freedom every day to be unholy. I am not talking about being perfect, but I am talking about being righteous for Christ. The second part which denies hell, is an attack on the Word of God. So clearly you can see in both of these statements that this person is not a true Christian but has instead created a form of self-religion to fit his purposes, his created reality. He will be left outside the gate if he does not accept the truth.

6.   You don't have to repent to anyone, just stop doing whatever it is you were doing

This is a subtle way of denying the Truth. I say subtle because this person is trying to acknowledge that a change in behavior is needed, so it counterfeits the truth by making us think: "oh yeah, we should stop such and such," but the way Satan uses this man, who calls himself a Christian, just to be clear, is to then say, "but you don't need to repent." Now let's think about this; what if you know this doesn't sound right, but you don't know why. We are going to problem solve here using the Bible but not referencing a scripture. This is a way you can look at a situation and come to the correct conclusion if you don't have a Bible available and don't know the scripture. Here is how we solve that, who taught repentance in the Bible. To be fair, repent is in the Bible several times old and new, but who spent their whole ministry teaching repentance and then baptizing people? John the Baptist, right? John the Baptist had a purpose in his life - teach people repentance to prepare the Way for Jesus. John the Baptist baptized Jesus. So, if Jesus went to John the Baptist and was baptized by Him, it stands to reason, Jesus endorsed John's teaching so repentance must be a requirement. Not to mention it is an overall teaching of the Bible both Old and New Testament. If you can't quote a scripture, but you are put on the spot, answer that way.

7. I've never felt God's presence, never had a single prayer answered, never got healed of anything, never heard his voice at all. The hypocrisy of churches full of unloving Christians, and abuse of churches. The Bible full of contradictions and absurdities and is just fiction. I question why did God not do more to help the people believe? Why did God not show up more, do more?

Let me put this in context for you. This person was talking about how every time he tries to evangelize, this is what he hears in response. He spoke about one guy in particular who gave him these words as a response to why he walked away from the church. Again, I see these words above as an

80

excuse to live in sin rather than seek the Truth of the
Lord. When someone speaks in absolutes, that is a red
flag. When someone pushes everything back on God with
"it's God's fault," that is a red flag. One thing I want to point
out here. When the excuse of hypocrisy of churches, and
abuse of churches is used, we need to think about that. Satan
is the one who has corrupted our churches for sure. We
cannot deny that. To then have an argument to not attend
church because it is corrupted is how Satan makes truth out
of a situation which he corrupted. When there is truth
imbedded into what someone says, the rest of what they say
will be considered acceptable as truth because a part is
true. See how the Christian who is trying to evangelize is
then left questioning why did God not do more? Why did
God not show up more for this guy? That reasoning is
lunacy. The Christian allowed the enemy to deny the Truth,
and then he just accepted the lies of the non-believer. We
must be stronger than that. We shouldn't be evangelizing if
we don't even know God ourselves. You are setting yourself
up to be deceived. That's like me going out to people and
telling someone "man, have you completed an Iron man?
No? oh man, you gotta do it, it will change your life. The
training is intense, but once you get it , the race itself is a
breeze." Ok, I don't do Iron Mans; I will never do an Iron
Man, know nothing about what it takes to compete in
one. So, I have no business recruiting other people to run an
Iron Man when I don't know what I am talking about. New
believers do this a lot, and sometimes they are the only ones
who do this. But they end up getting skewered by people like
this guy because they are not grounded in the Word yet and
don't know how to respond or handle a situation like
this. We all should evangelize, but we need to be honest in
the situation and if you are in over your head, say, "Hey, I
don't know how to answer what you are saying, but I can find

someone who can, and I'll be back to with them to talk to you." Don't walk away dismayed yourself because you allowed someone else to rob you of the little truth you had.

Ok, now I want to tell you about a conversation I had this week. All of these stories I'm discussing were with people who call themselves Christian just to make sure you understand the context. The initiator of this conversation, we'll call her Jane, calls herself a Christian but does not believe in Jesus and stated she does not believe in the crucifixion or the resurrection. Just to be clear, we are not talking about someone who is Jewish just to be clear. Jane is a "Christian" and is spreading the message of "God is love, and He loves everyone" and the initial comment she made was, "We need to respect everyone because religion is a personal thing, and it is intertwined with culture and family. We can all learn from each other and grow in understanding no matter what we believe." I'm not sure what happened before my arrival for her to make that statement. I was late in the conversation, but the first response I heard was a guy questioning her about where she derived her New Age, Satanic doctrine. I was a little shocked at how blunt he was, but I was interested to hear Jane's response. His point was - hey you are saying something to Christians, essentially telling us to quiet down the truth, and he was calling her on it. I have to commend him for that. He was clear, direct and said why he was saying what he was saying. As you can imagine, it didn't go over well with Jane, but that's where truth was revealed. What came out of Jane's mouth after that was all the satanic beliefs she was carrying. Because she got upset, the words coming out of her were satanic, and she was twisting the Bible by saying there are other ways to God, the Bible is not the only source of truth and much worse statements I don't want to repeat. You get the idea without me having to speak what she was saying. Once Jane was denying that Jesus died on the cross, another woman very calmly and very clearly explained the crucifixion and the resurrection to her. But Jane dismissed this well laid out explanation from this woman by calling her a legalist and told her to stop spreading her lies. That's where I stepped in and said that what this woman said was truth - not legalism. Which then meant she was now focused on me. I don't mind that; we must support truth to our brothers and sisters but do so without attacking. Jane tells me with attitude, "Yeah sure, your truth is the Bible's truth." I'm not sure what that meant, but I just responded, "Not sure why you are giving me attitude, but yes, my truth is in the Bible's truth. That should not bother you." Then she tells me my response is what is wrong with the world today. She then claimed she wasn't trying to give me an attitude. I responded telling her that the issue has nothing to do with the world, but it was her attitude and the way she chose to use her words. Note that how Jane initiated the conversation by telling us we needed to respect everyone because religion is a personal thing, and then she invalidates her own statement. Once her words became words that denied the truth of the Bible, she became more direct in what she was really saying, what she really intended and her real motive. Why call yourself a "Christian" if you do not believe in Jesus, do not believe in the truth of the Bible, believe there are ways to God other than Jesus and are socializing in Christian circles? Why? The true reason is the enemy is using her to create confusion, doubt, and to interfere in our relationship with the Lord. Don't feel that because you are in church or among people who call themselves Christian, that the enemy is not at work.

The Lord showed me how important it is for true believers to speak the truth when we are hearing otherwise. We will be held accountable for what we do or don't do for the Kingdom. We don't need to argue. We don't have to convince anyone of anything. We must get over wanting to win the argument. We may not be the one chosen to bring that particular person to the truth of Jesus. We may be just one of the other farmers there to plant the seed or water the seed or trim out some weeds or other pests. It may be for someone else to harvest. Speak the truth of Jesus but don't argue, don't get upset, and don't behave in a way Jesus would look at you and say, "That wasn't necessary. That's not My way." What happened in the Garden of Gethsemane when Peter cut off the ear of the guard there to arrest Jesu? Jesus didn't celebrate with Peter; no, he chastised him. We don't need to let everyone walk over us but we need to stand up and speak the truth. If it is accepted then great. If it is not, you did what is required of you so let the Lord handle the rest.

I want to switch gears a bit and talk to you about the Garden Tomb. I was there in February 2023, and it was amazing. Now this is the tomb that is widely believed to be the tomb owned by Nicodemus where Jesus was laid to rest. Of course, there is another huge tourist attraction that claims to be the place, and I went there too, but this is the garden tomb not far from Skull Hill where the crucifixion took place. While it is also a very busy tourist attraction, we were able to experience it twice, and I really want to share that with you. The first time we went to the Garden Tomb we were with a lot of people, there are tour groups in and out. It's crowded, and you have limited time in the actual tomb, seven seconds to be exact. The interest is so great, the facility wants to make sure everyone gets a chance to see and experience everything. At the same time this is not so great if you want to have a moment and experience "The

Experience" of a lifetime! The first day there was good, but I admit I walked away disappointed at being so ushered and rushed in and out of the tomb. Seven seconds goes pretty quick and even once you step out you need to move out of the way. Not exactly spiritual. Again, I totally understand, it's exciting to see so many people coming from all over the world just to be there for their seven seconds. Most people were fine with seven seconds; it truly is an empty tomb so there isn't anything to see, thankfully. Skull Hill, same thing, it is not what you expect as it is part of the modern city due to the bus depot being there where the crucifixion took place. It wasn't on top of the hill like you see in all the depictions. Anyhow, we left, got in the bus and as we were driving away, we realized my husband had lost his cell phone. When you are in a foreign country, the last thing you want to do is lose your cell phone. However, if you are going to lose it, a great place to lose it is at the Garden Tomb. We had no idea where we lost it, but we knew that it was turned in before we even knew we lost it. It was turned in and sitting there at the checkout while we were still in the giftshop buying our souvenirs. When our tour guide called the Garden Tomb as we were driving past it to leave, we were so relieved to find out it was in their hands and made a plan to go back the next morning to get it. The greatest thing that could have happened to us was to lose that phone. We went back the next morning just after they opened and because it was early, there was no one else there but the employees. We didn't even see the volunteers since tour buses wouldn't arrive until a few hours later. Being there early allowed us to spend an hour at Skull Hill, just sitting there imagining it, and seeing it after reading about it so many times; it was so peaceful and yet obnoxiously loud because it is a bus depot. It felt dismissed. I was able to journal there and enjoy the time in a way that was impossible the day before. From

Skull Hill to the Garden Tomb is a short walk through a garden area. At the tomb, we had another hour of peace and had the tomb all to ourselves. I was able to go in and sit and spend as much time in there as I wanted. We could feel the Holy Spirit there throughout our time. When I first walked into the tomb, I could feel the Holy Spirit, and as I stepped inside, my right knee buckled. My knees don't buckle. I could feel a presence there, and I was so appreciative of Him. I couldn't help but wonder what happened in that cave over during those three days or however many hours transpired. He was in there and then he arose; there had to have been such celebration in heaven, waiting, joy, tears. I wondered, how did He feel waking up in the tomb knowing He completed what His father asked of Him. Was he groggy at first, was he sore, so many questions! If you want to see the tomb and experience what I am talking about, we have a video up on the YouTube Channel: Life Journey with Dawn Simmons. We focus on Biblical locations on our trips and bring it all back to share with people so others can be there too, even if it's only through our lens.

"Deniers" may have infiltrated the Christian faith, but being at the location where the crucifixion and the resurrection occurred gives you a great sense of gratitude and appreciation of what occurred almost 2000 years ago. No one can honestly dispute that the event of the crucifixion took place; it is historically accurate and documented in sources outside of the Bible. Even "Deniers" will admit the resurrection took place, but they will degrade and try to cast aside the importance in order to pull us away from the saving grace of a salvation in Jesus. Don't be a Denier. If you deny Him, one day you will hear the words, "Away from Me, I never knew you."

Chapter 9

How Demons Work to Control Us

I want to discuss how demons work to control us and provide proven useful techniques that will serve to not only provide defensive power, but give you offensive power in the name of Jesus. We will examine one process of control Satan uses against us for his purposes. Specifically, we will be examining how possessiveness, manipulation, and dominance all work together to bring us to a place where Satan controls the incomes and outcomes of our lives. I'll also share some of my experiences working with a young man who has allowed Satan to control him but is trying to regain his life with Jesus.

Let's first examine control and apply the concepts we discussed in Chapter 6, What Are Demon Groupings? If for some reason you have skipped over that section, go back and read that before proceeding here because it lays groundwork that is really important to understand. One thing I did discuss in that chapter, and I want to bring up, is that demons function as experts or specialists, in a particular area. In the area of control, the demon of control will get some help in possessiveness, manipulation, and dominance from other demons that frequently are associated with insecurity, sadness, fear, inferiority, rejection, accusation, guilt, and anger may make an appearance but not always.

In the beginning of the process of control, demons will seek to be very possessive over someone. I don't mean possess; I mean to behave possessively towards the person. This can be done by creating a false sense of comfort. A familiar spirit is particularly well equipped for this role. In many cases, a feeling of possessiveness from the enemy is welcomed because the person has encountered rejection and may feel inferior and insecure. The moment the person feels a sensation of something, no matter what it is, wanting to be possessive over them - that sensation is wrongly interpreted as love. The blinders are being put on the person through this one act of possessiveness. The income sensations is manifested as a comfort which begins through manipulation. A counterfeit of love begins to permeate the landscape of the heart and mind of the individual. If you are wondering how this could possibly happen, think of how many people are truly starved for affection, devotion, true love in their lives, not just romantic love. Many times, their childhood lacked the support and love one would ideally receive from one's parent. A marriage or relationship is torn apart in their childhood. Have you ever met someone who goes from relationship to relationship and cannot be alone? Those weaknesses are being exploited, and the deception has created a counterfeit love to open the door for additional demons to enter this vulnerable individual. These demons begin to plant their seeds of doubt and fear and the spirit of paranoia frequently joins the group. The outcome is this person begins to pull back from usual social circles and is instead accompanied by all the demons for emotional support. This begins subtly to pull the person into a sense of safety, but in reality, the noose is being placed to begin to remove the life they have left and begin the stages of bondage. The use of manipulation to create this atmosphere is done with precision until they have achieved complete domination. The demons have successfully created the problem they intend to exploit.

The use of control against us cripples our minds and our hearts. Our bodies soon follow. Why is this so important? The enemy needs to strip you of your free will in order to get you positioned to accept what will ultimately happen when you are completely dominated. I know this sounds dark, I hate that this is so dark, but I want to tell you all these things so you will never end up here, without the light, without the Holy Spirit to overcome the darkness with you. I recently worked with a young man, let's call him John, who was completely controlled by the demonic. Every aspect of John's life was in bondage. The demons had already done so much damage that his mind only had moments of clarity to acknowledge and describe what was happening. He asked for help to be rid of these demons, and he asked for it to happen within a few days. John is easily the most severe case of demonization I have ever seen or of which I have any personal knowledge.

As we began to talk during our second meeting, John was intermittently clear minded. The more we discussed and identified specific demons the more erratic his thoughts, his speech and his body became. The prework I require for a deliverance session, he did not bring. The team was assembled however, and the Lord said to continue so I began to ask questions. I was trying to discern who the strongman was and all the others who were demonizing him. At no point was John in complete control of his mind. He would move in and out of answers that made no sense to the average person. Understand that to others John just looked like someone who was not very social, nervous, stressed, just a little different. There was nothing physically wrong with him. The more we talked, demons were being identified, and we could see distinct physical reactions to their identification. John walked through all the steps to move forward in evicting these demons. Understand I do nothing lightly, and John's safety is always most important as is the safety of my team. Also, on my team and present is a licensed behavioral health specialist. Thankfully, several demons were evicted with John's help. I will generally try to keep a record for the person I am working with, but it was impossible in this case. It was very a difficult, long process and the more progress we made, the more difficult it became; the resistance grew stronger. Listen to me - please listen to me. If you understand nothing else in this entire chapter, please understand this: You have got to hold onto your heart - you have got to maintain control of your mind. 1 Peter 5:8 tells us, *'be alert and of sober mind. Your enemy the devil prowls around like a roaring lion looking for someone to devour.'* Never submit to anyone but the Holy Spirit, Jesus, or God. Build your mind of Christ and protect it in the name of Jesus. It is so valuable to Jesus and sometimes we don't understand how valuable.

If you fall, and find yourself in sin, GET UP. Get up and get back to the Lord. The torment I saw in John you do not want. If you don't know how to get back up, reach out for help, a pastor, a friend you can trust; keep reaching and never give up. I want no one to endure what I saw happening with John. 1 John 5:19 tells us, *'We know that we are children of God, and that the whole world is under the **control** of the evil one'* but we are not the world, we are not under the control of the evil one unless we quit protecting our own house. 1 Thessalonians 4:4, tells us *'that each of you should learn to **control** your own body in a way that is holy and honorable'*. Most who read this think it only means restrictions. This is the lie Satan wants us to believe, because the truth is by living with control of our bodies and minds, we will live in freedom, the freedom of Jesus and not the bondage of the enemy. The spirit of control has a long and far reach once it gains dominance. The key to freedom is to recognize the signs and symptoms before dominance occurs.

I want to switch gears a little and talk about manipulation. The main tool used in manipulation is guilt. It keeps our wounds alive, and demons will keep pressing into it. The pressing methods can be both direct and subtle. Demons cannot directly come at someone to manipulate them each time and be successful, the process has to change periodically. For the demons to be successful over us, they must give the person a false sense of security and then begin to move in with subtle advances to manipulate and bring the person to their knees. Regardless of the conversations or interactions, the guilt tool will always come back around so that the person is never truly free. There are false senses of freedom, but there is always a noose present to yank them back in line periodically and remind them of their bondage of sadness, fear, insecurity, and inferiority. It doesn't start out this way but that is the dark hole you are being taken into slowly. The person will soon lose perspective. He or she will soon not see light as the darkness slowly pervades their mind. The idea is the dark is meant to overtake the mind so that soon you will only recognize darkness and will find comfort and solace in what you know and are becoming familiar with. Through that process the person will become a slave. The bondage will not end. It is similar to King Zedekiah with his eyes being gouged out as he was led away in chains to Babylon, and you soon know nothing but the bondage. This is where Satan seeks to take you in their domination.

Being possessive and manipulative are controlling activities, but domination is where the act of control eclipses all else, and the person is no longer able to think clearly for themselves. Demons will let you function for the most part in your life, but you may not be able to keep a job, keep your marriage, or worst of all keep yourself together. We have all seen people on the streets talking to themselves and seemingly living in another world. If we don't keep our house in order and keep control of our minds, chaos, confusion and despair is the end result. It will wreck you financially, emotionally, physically and intellectually. You ultimately lose your soul.

Back to John, he was specifically dealing with issues of sadness, nervousness, paranoia, confusion, tension, sexual sin, with anger appearing at times. There were many more, but these were the ones driving most of the behaviors and were controlling him. There were several manifestations of the demonic presence which would change depending on who was in control. I want you to understand that while John's level of control and demonization is extreme, it is present in our lives, our friends' lives, our church friends' lives more than you realize. Satan is out there to what? Well, Jesus told us the devil is out *"to steal, kill and destroy."* If you had even one of these areas to contend with, you would have real difficulty. We know that you will likely, I mean the chances are so rare that I can't even name a number statistically, but you will likely never have just one demon attacking you. John's story hasn't ended yet. Unfortunately, John isn't yet willing to give up everything. John also had familiar spirits that he would not let go of in order to be free. We won't go deep into a discussion of familiar spirits, but here are a few key points:

- The first way familiar spirits attempt to integrate is more difficult to discern.
- The familiar spirit uses deception by appearing to be a good companion or providing some sort of benefit or useful information.
- Many confuse this with the Holy Spirit and are led away from the Lord because they are not knowledgeable in the Word and not using discernment.

Familiar spirits use manipulation the same way other demonic spirits do. In this case, because John is not married, they are providing companionship. It's not a healthy companionship, but if John won't let them go, the demons get to stay. One interesting thing I want to point out in this case with John. Usually when a familiar spirit uses a person we know, it's a person who has passed. With John, it was all people who were still alive, but he thought were visiting him. Very uncommon. They can also pose as pets or appear to be superheroes or fantastical creatures to gain our interest.

So where do we go from here? You now know about John and his difficult battle to regain control. We need to do as Peter advised us and be alert and of sober mind. Paul tells us in 2 Corinthians 2:16 *'But we have the mind of Christ'*. Make sure you do - truly make sure you do. How are you handling demonic influences coming at you? Are you rebuking them immediately? Are you pondering on them a while? If you aren't rebuking them immediately you are beginning to play with fire. You have the matches in your hand essentially. We are in the battle whether we recognize it or not. The supernatural doesn't exist only when we can see it.

Let's go through some techniques you can use that will serve to not only to give you defensive power but give you some offensive power in the name of Jesus. We are talking about using your authority here.

1.   Rebuke in the name of Jesus. If this is all you can do, this is a good start to building up a defense. As soon as you have any sense of something coming at you to tempt or attack or manipulate you, simply say, "I rebuke that in the name of Jesus." Think of it like tennis, be like Serena and when it's coming at you - rebuke. It will come back at you again another way, rebuke it again. Just keep rebuking and eventually the enemy will realize it needs to move on, and you can celebrate like Serena!

2.   Add scripture to your rebuke. These are easy ones to remember and pull out of your mind quickly. If this is all you can do, this is a good start to building up your offense.

a.   Isaiah 54:17, *No weapon formed against me shall prosper*

b.   Luke 10:19, I *have given you authority to trample on snakes and scorpions and to overcome all the power of the enemy; nothing will harm you.*

c.   Romans 14:11, *As surely as I live, says the Lord, every knee will bow before me; every tongue with acknowledge God.*

d.   Romans 16:20, *The God of peace will soon crush Satan under your feet.*

3.   Give thanks to the Lord. A thankful heart is a protected heart. This will begin the process of creating an atmosphere around you that will over time keep the enemy

from wanting to be near you, and he will move on, away from you.

a.   1 Corinthians 15:57, *Thanks be to God! Gives us the victory through our Lord Jesus Christ.*

b.   1 Thessalonians 5:18, *In everything give thanks: for this is the will of God in Christ Jesus concerning you.*

c.   1 Chronicles 16:8, *Give praise to the Lord, proclaim His name; make known to the nations what He has done.*

d.   Psalms 100:4, *Enter his gates with thanksgiving and his courts with praise: give thanks to Him and praise His name.*

4.   Scriptures to build up your strength. Adding this will position you not only to keep your house clean but help someone else with their house.

a.   Ephesians 6:10-17 – The Armor of God

i. Finally, be strong in the Lord and in his mighty power. Put on the full armor of God, so that you can take your stand against the devil's schemes. For our struggle is not against flesh and blood, but against the rulers, against the authorities, against the powers of this dark world and against the spiritual forces of evil in the heavenly realms. Therefore put on the full armor of God, so that when the day of evil comes, you may be able to stand your ground, and after you have done everything, to stand. Stand firm then, with the belt of truth buckled around your waist, with the breastplate of righteousness in place, and with your feet fitted with the readiness that comes from the gospel of peace. In addition to all this, take up the shield of faith, with which you can extinguish all the flaming arrows of the evil one. Take the helmet of salvation and the sword of the Spirit, which is the word of God.

b.   Psalms 31:3

  i. Since you are my rock and my fortress, for the sake of your name lead and guide me.

c.   Job 42:2

  i. I know you can do all things; no purpose of yours can be thwarted.

d.   Joshua 23:14

  i. You know with all your heart and soul that not one of all the good promises the Lord your God gave you has failed. Every promise has been fulfilled; not one has failed.

These scriptures are just to get you something easy to have readily available. A scripture journal is an even better way to start building up your weapons to start conquering our unseen enemies. Take control, take authority and take ownership of what you need to do to give the Holy Spirit the access and ability to move in your life the way He wants to and give you the life of abundance He promised.

Chapter 10

Four Tactics Satan uses to Manipulate Us

To fully embrace *Conquering Our Unseen Enemies*, we need to go deeper into enemy tactics of manipulation and discuss four ways the enemy works to manipulate believers in our day to day lives. Many of the topics we have and will examine here seem separate and apart from our day to day lives because of the severity of what we are examining. There are other tactics the enemy uses that are subtle, like a slow burn. We may miss these tactics as we go about our daily tasks focused on all we need to get done in our day. What we are examining here are very common issues we need to be aware of, so we are able to identify and stop these tactics against us immediately.

Let's start off talking about how Jesus describes Satan. In John 8:44, Jesus is in Jerusalem speaking to the Pharisees, religious leaders. *"You belong to your **father**, **the** devil, and you want to carry out your **father**'s desires. He was a murderer from **the** beginning, not holding to **the** truth, for **there** is no truth in him. When he **lies**, he speaks his native language, for he is a liar and **the father of lies**."* Satan, the father of lies, is at the root of all the enemy tactics. When the root is a lie, everything he produces is a lie.

This week I was talking with a man, we will call him John, and we were developing a prayer action plan over his daughter. The daughter is currently in an involuntary psychiatric hold and is saying some extremely demonic things right now with brief moments of clarity. Those brief moments gave John hope. At times, the daughter will claim to be Jesus. Those type of behaviors are easy to recognize, but understanding that it is the Spirit of the Anti-Christ working is what we may miss. The demonic spirit is skilled at using the right words some days to her to get her to believe she is Jesus. Other times, there are some more subtle comments made that confuse John. He wants to try to figure out what she is talking about. There were multiple accusations made against family members and friends, but they were just accusations, and there is no way to verify the truth in any of the accusations. I could see how it was upsetting to John, and he was questioning if the accusations being asserted were true of the various family members and friends. We must remember in all situations where the enemy is working against us that we cannot trust in what is being said. We don't want to take an accusation and act on it based only on that circumstance. Satan is our accuser, and what he does is all rooted in lies. This is not to say some accusations are not true, but we can't act on accusations given to us in this way.

In John's situation, he had a wide spectrum of demonic words spoken so there was no mistaking the enemy was at work. For us, in our day to day lives, it will be more subtle and because we are distracted, we may miss that it is actually the enemy behind these simple things, and tactics that begin to manipulate us.

So let's talk about four tactics the enemy uses every day to manipulate us with lies. We will see what the Bible reveals as the truth we need to live by in our lives. Life is found in truth and truth is found in life.

1.   Eroding our confidence through doubt and fear

The spirit of doubt has a purpose to deceive us into questioning our decisions and actions. The goal is to lead us into inactivity. Doubt erodes trust. Doubt destroys creativity. Doubt builds walls. Doubt shuts doors. Doubt ends friendships. Doubt ends businesses. Doubt breaks contracts. Doubt builds fears. Doubt conceals talent. Doubt shreds love.

The Spirit of Doubt is dangerous because it is a counterfeit to logic and reason. The Spirit of Doubt works quietly. It doesn't show up in your face, instead it slowly makes its way toward you taking every opportunity to exploit your struggles into its advantage. It waits for a moment of weakness or takes the time to carefully craft circumstances to get you to a moment of uncertainty, and then it begins to use your own words and thoughts against you. If we cannot maintain the integrity of our faith and recognize when the enemy is coming at us, it will crumble, it will be eaten away and what will you have left to stand on for support? Faith in our walk with Jesus is vital to our life in Jesus. We have to protect our minds and hearts; we have to protect our faith. The opposite of doubt is faith. Faith can hold you up through all things. Faith can build you up in your hardest days. Faith can tear down the plans of the enemy.

In Matthew 14:31, Peter is walking in faith and gets out of the boat, but loses focus for a second. We see Jesus respond in this way; *immediately Jesus reached out his hand and caught him. "You of little faith," he said, "why did you doubt?"*

Our faith must be bigger than what the enemy is driving toward us. Our level of faith is a choice we make because of our relationship with Jesus. Doubt will only lead you to fear. When we act in fear, we make poor choices. Never let the circumstances you see, dictate your outcome.

2.   Using our past against us with guilt and shame

Once you become saved and born again, the Bible tells us that we have now become new creations in Jesus Christ. Our past is no longer our past in Christ's eyes. He never will bring up your past as a way to lead you forward. He will guide you away from the ways of your past without bringing shame. We must learn to let our past go. If we cannot do that then we are telling Jesus what He did on the cross is not good enough. We can learn a lot from our past. Our past can help lead others by your example, but we don't look back at it and let it hinder us from our future in Him.

The enemy will use our past to bring out our shame and guilt to keep us from doing anything for the Kingdom because you don't want others to know about our past. I know with some couples who are in second marriages, the shame of a divorce can be something the enemy uses to create a feeling that others are condemning them. Unfortunately, the enemy will use Christians against each other in this way. You don't see it often, but I've seen it recently. It was the enemy using a spirit of religion residing in another Christian to attack a number of people in second marriages. I had a pastor in the past who would not perform any weddings where either person was entering into a second marriage. There was not an attempt to understand the circumstance and to evaluate each situation individually before deciding if he would be involved in performing the ceremony. The pastor had a blanket belief that second marriages are not biblical. Again, the enemy using the Spirit of Religion to create an environment to create hurt in those Christians who were in second marriages. Whether they were biblical divorces or were even saved at the time of the divorce or after the divorce - none of that mattered. Jesus did not condemn or create hurt in that way. He used truth to lead someone the right direction, toward Him. In contrast, the enemy creates divides and leads us away from Him through hurt tied to guilt and shame.

The Holy Spirit we have as believers also works differently in us than do the tactics of the enemy. The Holy Spirit uses conviction in our hearts to lead us from our sinful life, no matter how big or small, toward Him. He does not use shame or guilt, but rather He uses His right and true ways to lead us to repentance and back in relationship and fellowship with him. Guilt or shame is not His way. He encourages and uses His loving ways to guide us on the right path.

If you have something that still hangs in the back of your mind, get rid of it. Give it to the Lord. Don't give the enemy anything to work with in coming against you.

3.   Using others against us with lies, jealousy, and paranoia

Remember, Jesus calls Satan, the Father of Lies so Satan will readily use this as a way to get to us and break us apart in our hearts. We, unfortunately, don't think in terms of first judging or evaluating what words are spoken to us before accepting them. We don't go around and question everything everyone says to us to ensure accuracy, so it's not something we think to do when the enemy is using lies to come against us.

Do you know one of the reasons Americans are such easy targets abroad for scams? I think Canadians fall into this category as well. When we travel abroad to other countries, in our culture we have more of a tendency to think people are going to act and treat us the way we are used to acting and treating people. As if others will think the same way we do and will act accordingly. As an American, I think we have a reputation for being overly sensitive to offending others, so we tend to be very nice. Very naïve. Not all Americans, I have seen plenty of ignorant, rude, embarrassing Americans when I travel and it's all you can do to try to counteract that entitled behavior. Okay that was me digressing, back to the subject matter at hand. Americans can be seen as being too nice and therefore easy to be taken advantage of in order to separate us from our money. Our niceness or naivety gets used against us. Now we have plenty of people in every country that are willing to take advantage of us, but it's just a known tactic because it works. I have found Europeans are more aware, more savvy in that regard which is likely due to their culture and their history. The enemy will work the same way, exploiting our weakness against us because we generally aren't expecting it.

Jealousy is a tactic used to attack our self-worth. It affects how we view others, the world, creates bitterness, harbors hatred, entices people to compromise their morals, and only serves to take us into a downward spiral that will ultimately produce rejection in our lives. All of that has an origin and it is all from Satan.

We only need to go to Genesis 4 to see the first murder committed out of jealousy. In Genesis 4:7 we see God warning Cain, *"If you do what is right, will you not be accepted? But if you do not do what is right, sin is crouching at your door; it desires to have you, but you must rule over it."* Cain could not do what is right, and he murdered his brother, Abel. I doubt Abel ever expected that. No one had ever murdered anyone at that time and truly most people would never think of such an act, but for Cain, it was his answer to his jealousy, and it was done by the influence of Satan. Notice that God tells Cain he must rule over the affects of jealousy. As early as we can trace our history, we have had authority over Satan. We just choose to often to not use it.

Paranoia, fed by jealousy, will break you down mentally, and you will end up trusting no one. That will tear apart your relationship with the Lord. Which leads us to our next tactic.

4.   Addiction Issues

Addiction issues run far and wide. This goes beyond the obvious and observable involving drugs or alcohol. There are a lot of other unspoken addictions or rarely recognized behaviors we do that are truly addictions.

Why are addiction issues so damaging to us? Aside from the consequences a lot of addiction issues present - there are underlying issues. Addiction extends to other areas we don't always acknowledge: E-cigarettes, going to the gym, shopping, sports, television, gaming or work. On the surface, many of these seem like a non-issue, but when we move to a place of needing that addiction to function or where it takes over our time in such a way that it interferes with our time with the Lord, then we have a problem we need to address. We don't want to have anything that becomes an idol or any area where we can't function unless we have that one thing in our life when that one thing is clearly not a necessity. If we can't turn it off and walk away, then we need to ask ourselves if this is an addiction. Does it take up our thoughts and drive our behaviors is a good way to gauge if we have an addiction.

Those are the top four areas of manipulation I tend to see people struggle with the most. If any of those resonate with you, rebuke it, kick it to the curb and focus on what the Lord has planned for you. Now let's move on to how to stop these tactics from working on us. I have four simple steps for that.

Four Steps to Stop Enemy tactics

1.   Identify It: what occurred, what did the Holy Spirit reveal, how does it line up with the Bible or the character of God?

2.   Rebuke It: we always want that to be an immediate response when we begin to see the enemy is involved anywhere we are. It's as simple as saying: "I rebuke that in the name of Jesus."

3.   Root it Out: what triggered it to influence you, is it something from your past, is it something that happened to you that you have held on to, how did it get to you (what path did it take – person, location, etc?)

4.   Give it to the Lord and speak Truth over your life: Once we have identified what it is and you have rooted out why it is being used against you, hand it over to the Lord. This is a good time to quote a scripture such as: *"no weapon formed against me shall prosper"* Isaiah 54:17. Rarely is the second part of this sentence quoted but it really applies well here *"and you will refute every tongue that accuses you."* Rephrased I would say, No weapon formed against me shall prosper, and

I will refute every tongue that accuses me. That's the rebuke part for our purposes.

Find your own scriptures, find your own words that fit you, just find the words and follow through on taking authority over the enemy using these tactics on you.

Part Three:

Demonic Spirits

Chapter 11

Doubt

We examined about the Spirit of Doubt briefly in the last chapter, but we are going to dig deeper into the Spirit of Doubt in Part III as we discuss specific demons. Satan and his demons use the Spirit of Doubt to deceive us into questioning our decisions and actions to lead us into inactivity. We are going to go more in depth into doubt and then talk about the role of faith in *Conquering Our Unseen Enemies* of Doubt.

The spirit of Doubt is a creeper spirit. It doesn't show up in your face; instead, it slowly makes its way toward you taking every opportunity to exploit challenges around you to its advantage. It waits for a moment of weakness or takes the time to carefully craft circumstances to get you to a moment of weakness, and then it begins to use your own words and thoughts against you. Doubt takes both innocent and mean-spirited words or actions from others which are both unintended and/or intended and which have been spoken or directed toward you and twists them to create new meaning. The purpose of this twist is for the demon to turn the words and actions back at you with the intention of attacking your heart and mind. You don't see it coming because it uses disguises making it appear circumstances are against you, when in fact nothing of the kind exists. Normal challenges have been magnified and twisted to deceive you into doubting yourself and eroding trust in others, including the Lord, but it was all carefully crafted out of lies and deception.

The Spirit of Doubt is dangerous because it is a counterfeit to logic and reason. It will use what you think is your God given ability to discern and will counterfeit your process of decision making to drive you to do nothing, rather than move forward. The Spirit of Doubt makes you think you are better off in your comfort zone, that no one will listen to you, that no one cares, that you cannot do what God has, in truth, given you the ability to do with the gifts he has already given you for use in His Kingdom and for His glory.

Doubt will frequently be the strongman, the leader, in demonization.

The Spirit of Doubt will parade alongside you as support, silently waiting for the moment to tell you how weak you are and pull you down. In parading as support, it can build a relationship with you in the hope you will listen to the Spirit of Doubt and believe it is trying to keep you safe and away from rejection or from being hurt. In those moments as it suspends you in doubt, it is opening the backdoor to your mind and heart and quietly waving in other demonic influences to come on in and get situated. With Doubt as the strongman, getting rid of him is incredibly difficult because the person in doubt will question everything during the eviction process and that questioning allows that spirit as the strongman to remain.

So why does it work so well? It specializes as all demons do, but it specializes at worm holing its way through our faith. If we cannot maintain the integrity of our faith, it will crumble, it will be eaten away and then what will you have left to stand on for support? Faith in our walk with Jesus is crucial. We have to protect our house; we have to protect our faith. No believer has ever had a life where their faith wasn't challenged. We need, to a certain degree, to be challenged for our faith to build. Once we see victory after victory, we get stronger, but still, most of us deal with that Spirit of Doubt somewhere in our life. Once it has creeped into one area of our lives, it moves into the other areas, and we will see downward changes happen in our marriage, in our work, in our relationships and most importantly, in our relationship with the Lord. For some, it seems like the whole world is coming down on them and they cannot understand it or seem to find a way out of it. Unfortunately for some, it will lead them to thoughts of harming themselves and of suicide. As a strongman, Doubt is incredibly powerful, and its aftermath can be devastating. Often, we think of the in-your-face demonic influences as the worst, but they are not. The in-your-face demons like anger, for example, are showing their colors then and there as they appear. You know they are there; they don't exactly have the ability to hide because their nature requires an activity on their part to be revealed. We generally know when someone is angry even when they try to hide it. Doubt on the other hand - Doubt hides, and we can even find ourselves playing into someone else's Spirit of Doubt and coming into agreement with them without realizing it.

Doubt erodes trust. Doubt destroys creativity. Doubt builds walls. Doubt shuts doors. Doubt ends friendships. Doubt ends businesses. Doubt breaks contracts. Doubt builds fears. Doubt conceals talent. Doubt shreds love.

Now that we are clear on who Doubt is, have a better understanding of how strong Doubt can be, and can

111

recognize the amount of destruction it is capable of rendering in our lives, what now?

We have briefly discussed the opposite of doubt is faith. I want to talk to you about faith. We are now going to revisit the story of my son and his stroke. His story is part of my story and always will be. I want you to know that I am where I am because I've had to walk through fire. I've been in the desert; I've had to use spiritual warfare to get the outcomes promised to me, and I want you to benefit from it and do the same in your life wherever and whenever you may need it. What I am going to share illustrates the Spirit of Doubt attacking me during an incredibly stressful time. This situation required a level of faith I had not needed to access before in my 50 plus years of life.

My journey starts with a YouTube video I did in February/March of 2022 year titled, *"3 examples of strength in the Lord."* In it I talk about Job, Peter and Joshua. The discussion on Peter centered around his faith and strength in getting out of the boat and walking on the water toward Jesus. I wondered to myself what would I do if I had a "getting out of the boat moment." What would a getting out of the boat moment look like today? I felt I'd had a lot of challenges in my life, some pretty serious, some not so much, but nothing that required me to have a walk on water type of faith and strength. Fast forward about four weeks later and I was working on a course I was about to record called *"Moving Mountains through Prayer.* Now this is not a commercial for either of the YouTube channel or the course, but it's important to the story. As I sat at the computer on a Sunday afternoon finalizing the course information, I got a text. My daughter in law was letting me know my son was in the ER, but it didn't seem like anything serious, she was just letting me know. I asked the Lord about it, and He said a few things I didn't yet understand, but what I did understand was that he said my son would survive, and he would be better than he was before. Looking back at that word should have registered with me a little more, but in the moment, since the Lord said he would survive, my thoughts went to "then it must not be anything I need to be concerned about." I glossed over the specifics the Lord gave me and went straight to what I wanted to hear. Within an hour, my daughter in law called, and she asked me to come to the ER. After I arrived, more tests revealed my son had a major stroke at some point within the last 12-24 hours, and the blood flow to his brain had already begun to shut down in two carotid arteries. He needed surgery immediately. He was then transferred to the stroke center at a hospital 10 minutes away. Because of the late hour and somewhat due to Covid restrictions we were still contending with in California, we were not allowed to go but we were told we could see him the next morning.

He had an MRI on that next morning, a Monday, and it confirmed the severity of the stroke and a plan for surgery was set which would occur Tuesday morning. Surgery on Tuesday went well, no complications, he was alert and able to move everything once he was awake. All seemed to have gone smoothly, and it was just about his recovery at this point. He was complaining a lot about pain, however, and nothing seemed to work to control the pain. We left him that night at 7:25, just after the shift change so that we could talk to the nurse who would be watching him throughout the night. We, my daughter in law and I, were not allowed to stay with him. As we left, I spoke to him, but he did not speak to me; he seemed different. I remember clearly how he seemed to be looking at me - but not looking at me. I thought the medications were finally giving him some peace. The new

113

nurse let us know she was changing his CT scan from the morning to that night so as we left, he was being taken away for the CT scan. They made sure they had our numbers and would call my daughter in law with the results. To this day, I will never forget the look, that distant look in my son's eyes.

We drove home; we only lived about a mile apart. I had just settled onto the couch and finished texting everyone to let them know the surgery was a success and thanking everyone for prayers. It was about 8:15. I sent the last text; I remember watching my arm as it came to rest on the couch still holding my phone, and it rings. My daughter in law was calling, and I answered the phone to "Dawn, we need to go back to the hospital, he is going back into emergency surgery, and they don't think he is going to make it."

This was not in alignment with what the Lord told me, so how could it be true? I couldn't deny what was happening in the natural, but how could it be true? Did something happen that allowed the enemy access to my son's life? It didn't matter. I stood in faith on what the Lord told me - that was my truth and that was my son's truth, no matter what the doctors thought or believed.

I began to act as we raced back to the hospital. Everyone I had just texted got a rather fervent phone call. If you were in my call list, well, you got a call too, as many as I could in the 10 minutes it took to get back to the ER. My daughter in law arrived at the hospital about the same time, and we were escorted from the ER to ICU by a security guard. He took us using a back way, the service elevator, so we were not familiar with the path we were on and not really even focused on the walk. We were going through the motions and didn't realize we were walking the opposite way into the ICU unit than we had walked into earlier in the day. Going this opposite way dropped us off almost directly at his room when we entered the ICU, which we were not expecting. The rooms were arranged in a semi-circle, and he was at the end of the semi-circle but coming in the opposite way, he was now at the beginning of the semi-circle, so we were not prepared for what we saw so immediately. Looking back, I don't know that we could have done anything differently to be prepared but nonetheless, we didn't have the walk we were expecting to try to prepare ourselves. As far as the doctors and nurses were concerned, he wasn't going to survive, and they were giving us our last minutes with him before he passed. He wasn't conscious; he was intubated; he looked lifeless. He was positioned to be taken to the OR for an emergency surgery that was expected to take six hours, but we were well advised they didn't expect him to make it. Again, that was not in alignment with what the Lord told me so I couldn't understand why we were here. I only knew I couldn't believe it: I wouldn't believe it, and I couldn't allow myself in any way to come into agreement with what the doctors were telling us. My daughter in law had held up well throughout this whole process but the shock of what we walked into was taking its toll. We came into agreement together and rebuked what the enemy was trying to do, and I prayed over my son from head to toe. The irony of my having just finished writing a course on *Moving Mountains through Prayer* was that here I was with this huge mountain that didn't belong. I didn't care what anyone else thought. My son was not dying that night. He was not dying from this, he was going to be better than he was before because that is what the Lord said, and the Lord only speaks truth. I stood there in that ICU room, and I stood in front of a mountain, but I prayed over my son with everything I had in me. I was loud and I only knew one thing - Jesus had the victory I needed, and I was

115

claiming it for my son. My daughter in law was worried I was too loud, but I told her we were bringing Jesus in this place, and everybody in ICU needed Jesus and kept going. It was actually a faith-based hospital, so prayer was pretty usual there. One of the doctors kept telling us what we should expect throughout the night, and he would end each sentence with "God willing." After a few times of hearing that, I started responding, "He is willing" just to make sure his tentative statement wasn't allowing doubt a foot in the door.

Nearly all the family in the area had arrived. The hospital waived their Covid restrictions, and we were all allowed into the ICU waiting room. We all settled in for a long night. We told stories of my son; we laughed; we cried; we prayed, and we cherished that time together. It wasn't pleasant by any means, but we were comforted by the Holy Spirit in that waiting room in ways I can't share. Doubt was not allowed to enter into our time that night.

Prior to the first surgery I told the Neurosurgeon, Dr Oni, the best brain surgeon in the world, that the Lord had specifically chosen him for this surgery. I had no idea if he is a believer. He looked perplexed when I said that but that's ok, it was true. The Lord showed me in a vision how His hands took over Dr Oni's hands as the surgery began, and then I could see the surgery begin. At the time the Lord showed me the vision, it was during the first surgery, but the position of my son in the vision was not the position for the first surgery so I was confused by my vision. As I waited during the second surgery, the Lord reminded me of the vision, and it made complete sense to me because it was the position revealed to me of my son in the second surgery.

My son made it through the surgery, he was critical for a week and remained in ICU for about three weeks. Then he transferred to the rehab unit. It wasn't easy - by no means was it easy. He had brain damage and that affects everything. I was there as he learned to walk again. I was there as he realized he was already married to his wife. I was there as he ate his first foods again; he really wanted Motts Apple Sauce. Today, he is considered a miracle by Dr Oni. He was back at work full time within 3 months, and he started to play golf again. This stroke happened in California, but he was in escrow on a house in Texas during all this and he was able to move into his new house in August. You would never know by looking at him or talking to him that any of this ever happened. That is the truth of Jesus. Faith can hold you up through all things. Faith can build you in your hardest days. Faith can tear down the plans of the enemy.

Let's see what the Bible says about doubt and faith using the story of Peter I referenced earlier. Here we have Peter responding to the Lord calling to him to come out to him on the sea and join him. Peter did, but then lost his faith, his focus for a moment. In Matthew 14:31 we see Jesus respond in this way, *immediately Jesus reached out his hand and caught him. "You of little faith," he said, "why did you doubt?"* As I waited for my son in the waiting room during that second surgery, the Lord let me know that it was my time, my Peter moment right there. Notice that Jesus immediately responded to Peter, and He will do the same for us. Also, notice that Peter was required to act in faith. If we let doubt win, we cripple our faith. It will inhibit our ability to reach for Jesus which is exactly what the enemy is counting on as our response. We must not waiver, but stand on our faith.

Let's look at another example Jesus gives us about faith and doubt. Matthew 21:21-22, Jesus replied, *"Truly I tell you, if you have faith and do not doubt, not only can you do what was done to the fig tree, but also you can say to this mountain, 'Go, throw yourself into the sea,' and it will be done. If you believe, you will receive whatever you ask for in prayer."*

Listen, doubt is one of the strongest of the demonic strongmen. Our faith must be bigger than the strongman and through Jesus, it can be. It is a choice we make because of our relationship with Jesus. Never let the circumstances you see, dictate your outcome. If Jesus had done that, how could He have been resurrected? That required faith on His part, but we never talk about the faith of Jesus, do we? He had to have faith in His Father or He would not have been able to do any of the miracles or stand up to the Pharisees or prevent a woman from being stoned just by His words. If you take nothing else away from this book, take with you the thoughts of Jesus and the level of faith He had to have to live out His life. If He can do it, so can we. He was human just as we are. Trust Him.

Chapter 12

Jealousy

Jealousy. We all know what jealousy is like. We have all had a
spirit of Jealousy, and it's likely we have all been the recipient
of some jealous ire from someone somewhere along the way.
It is an ugly, ugly emotion that gets its' start in the
beginning. Satan's own pride created a spirit of Jealousy of all
that God has and is, and as a result a spirit of rebellion
emerged against God. Therefore, God threw him out of
Heaven. We talked about it in Chapter Part One, but Satan's
jealousy is also illustrated in his interaction with Eve in the
Garden of Eden. He deceived her and used what people
today call FOMO (Fear of missing out) to play on her being
jealous of what God had, by not being allowed to eat from
the tree of knowledge of good and evil. You can find that
story in Genesis 2:16-17, and then the fall occurs in Genesis
3. We don't have to look any further than Genesis 4 to see
the first murder committed out of jealousy; we talked about
that in Chapter 10. In Genesis 4:7 we see God warning Cain,
*"If you do what is right, will you not be accepted? But if you do not do
what is right, sin is crouching at your door; it desires to have you, but you
must rule over it."* Cain could not do what is right and out of a
spirit of Jealousy, he murdered his brother, Abel.

Through the Bible we know that jealousy has been around
since before mankind existed and began in man from the
beginning of our existence. It creates division among

families, tears apart marriages, breaks down churches, ruins businesses and worst of all it has cost millions of people their lives. The Spirit of Jealousy is a root, and then it brings along other sins to create more chaos.

Jealousy is the 10th Commandment given to us by God. Exodus 10:17, *"You shall not covet your neighbor's house. You shall not covet your neighbor's wife, or his male or female servant, his ox or donkey, or anything that belongs to your neighbor."* Social media and reality TV have created an immediate avenue for jealousy as cars, houses and personal accessories have taken the place of the ox and the donkey. Almost all of us notice when our neighbor gets a new car. My neighbor just did earlier this year and yes, it is way sexier, way - way sexier than my car, but I don't want his car. I can appreciate the aesthetics of his car, but it ends there. When I look back at my car, I am perfectly happy with the decision I made when I bought my car. I think jealousy as a sin is often overlooked because it is the last of the commandments, the 10th, and people who are jealous think it doesn't directly harm another person or that anyone else can see their sin.

The Spirit of Jealousy attacks our self-worth, affects how we view others, the world, creates bitterness, harbors hatred, entices people to compromise their morals, and only serves to take us into a downward spiral that will ultimately produce rejection in our lives. All of that has an origin and it is all from Satan. We all have a weakness, all of us, and that is what will be exploited as often as possible and as severely as is necessary to get us to respond in a way not pleasing to the Lord. James 3:16 tells us this, *"For where you have envy and selfish ambition, there you find disorder and every evil practice."*

When we are in a situation and the Spirit of Jealousy is present, through our own experience, we know what to expect; we know how it feels when we are jealous. But how do we spot it when it is working against us in someone else? We know what it is, but we don't always recognize it when we come against it in someone else. Do we recognize it to be able to call it what it is? When you recognize it, you can defeat it, even when it is working in someone else against you.

Recognizing it comes down to characteristics. The characteristics of the Spirit of Jealousy are not always easy to spot at first, but once you pick up on one or two you will see how they weave together. You know you have someone with a Jealous spirit near you or who is creating an environment with a Spirit of Jealousy when you see any combination of these characteristics, particularly repeatedly. (One off may just be an unpleasant person.) A person with a Jealous Spirit will:

1) Ask you questions to make you feel uncomfortable or slight you in some way publicly or one on one in an attempt to tear apart your confidence.

2) Compliment you all the time, not genuinely, and they work it to be a backhanded compliment or raise themselves higher than you even in the compliment.

3) Make everything a competition and as result brag about their achievements. They cannot be happy about your success. They will say what you receive is due to luck - no acknowledgment of your work or effort.

4) Steal your successes which includes being a copycat in an attempt to present something as if it was theirs. Copy you in general.

5) Blow up your plans to try to sabotage you or lead you astray. This is usually done in a subtle way, so you won't pick up on what they are doing.

6) Always find a way to cut you off when you are speaking. The attempt is to diminish you to other people. This can even be done with body language like a simple eye rolling.

7) Put you down in front of people and will spread rumors about you with the intent to damage your credibility or reputation. The purpose is to bring you down below them.

8) Criticize everything you do in a way that is not constructive.

9) Flat out just do not like you. They are unable to speak in kindness to you and it's only you.

Now we have the characteristics identified. Let's look at how a Jealous spirit has behaved in some real-life examples, and then we will tackle how to evict this influence in your life.

This first example involves a woman we will call, Jane, who is dealing with a woman at her church who has been treating her differently than she treats others in their Bible Study. For ease of reference, we will refer to the person who is jealous in our scenarios as Jeal, as in Jealous. In this situation, Jane, was attending a Bible study group and a few weeks later Jeal joined. Jeal is about 20 years older than Jane. They did not know each other from church prior to this Bible Study. Both women have been Christians for a very long time, but Jane is more mature in her understanding of the Bible and the Holy Spirit and contributes to group discussion quite a bit. Each week Jane treats Jeal the same as everyone else, but during the Bible study Jane has noticed that Jeal will mumble under her breath while Jane is speaking and moves around when everyone else is sitting and paying attention. Those behaviors on their own may not mean anything but combined with a few additional things that have begun to happen, Jane feels Jeal's behavior is escalating. In front of the group, Jeal recently asked where Jane went to church, and then when Jane responded that she went to the same church (both women have been going to the same church for years), Jeal made a comment with a sneering attitude, "Well. I've never seen you there." Jane then replied with where she sat so she could see her at church the next week. Jeal responded that she never sits in the same place, she wants to keep moving around because then she feels more a part of the church. The way Jeal said it was as if Jane was lower than she, as if she was slighting Jane for sitting in the same place each week. Jane has picked up on looks she is being given but is choosing to ignore them. In the last week, Jane was advised by another person in the Bible study that when Jane was talking, Jeal was rolling her eyes, and asked Jane if something was going on to cause that type of noticeable reaction from Jeal.

In the next situation, different people with similar names, Jane 2, was hosting a Bible study in her home, and Jeal was new to the Bible study. It was a Bible study that allowed for a lot of discussion and functioned well before Jeal began to attend. Everyone in the Bible study has been a Christian for over 15 years. It was a loose agenda with each person bringing scriptures to talk about and share how it has affected them over the previous month. They met monthly. Jane 2 noticed after a few months that whenever she spoke, Jeal would then speak, and whatever Jeal said was amped one level up from whatever Jane 2 said. For two more months this behavior persisted. Jane 2 thought it seemed silly. She had to be misinterpreting Jeal, but Jane 2 went ahead and tested her theory and sure enough, no matter what Jane 2 said, Jeal told an even better story and was even trying to "teach" Jane 2 implying Jane 2 wasn't as knowledgeable as Jeal. Whatever Jane 2 said, Jeal had to "correct" her by adding information that was unrelated to what Jane 2 was discussing. An example of this was a discussion in the group of the Old Testament and Jeal added that she was teaching herself Hebrew and then added information to show her knowledge of Hebrew, was above everyone else.

On the third month, Jane 2 decided to switch things up in the hopes of putting an end to this behavior, so she let everyone else speak and then Jane 2 would go last. It was a change in their routine, but no one was bothered by it - except Jeal. Jane 2 described the look on Jeal's face when she changed the routine as lost; she didn't know what to talk about without having Jane 2's information to work from and challenge. After the meeting ended and everyone left, Jane 2 was on the phone. About ten minutes later, Jeal returned to Jane 2's home to tell her that what Jane 2 shared in the meeting, Jeal also had that same situation so she knew even more about it. She just wanted Jane 2 to know that, and then she left. Jane 2 was confused by that odd behavior. During all this time other things were happening as well. Jeal would ask Jane 2 if she knew where to find different passages in the Bible. Jeal on multiple occasions told Jane 2 that she was being told by the Lord that she needed to pray over Jane 2, implying she had some knowledge of Jane 2 from the Lord that Jane 2 did not have of herself. Jeal would continually talk about all she was doing for people and all the information the Lord was giving her over the future of the area. Jane 2 did take Jeal out to lunch in an attempt to develop the relationship and work it out, but during the lunch Jeal began to drill Jane 2 about her ministry gifts and her family history. Regardless of Jane 2's response, Jeal was always more advanced and experienced. Jane 2 stopped taking Jeal to lunch.

The third situation I want to share with you involves a work situation. John is a manager who relocated about 5 years ago to take this management position. One of the men who works for him, Jeal 2, wanted John's job, but he was not selected because he was not qualified. John was brought in to overhaul a department, and Jeal 2 had been part of the reason for the overhaul. Nonetheless, Jeal 2 immediately set up to be seen as John's "right hand man." John was aware Jeal 2 was not selected for the job and initially believed Jeal 2 was sincere at wanting to do his job well and supporting John, although he did express some bitterness over not being selected. Over time, John began to notice Jeal 2 would interrupt John at staff meetings, trying to take over presentations and assert himself as the person with the answers. John was also advised Jeal 2 was talking to other departments and taking credit for all the success that John was having in rebuilding the department. When John had to take a short medical leave due to an unexpected surgery, Jeal 2 packed up all of John's belongings and set himself up in John's office as if he was taking over. Six months later when John was given a promotion for the work he had done the previous years, Jeal 2 told John he was only promoted because of Jeal 2 stepping in for him while he was out for surgery. When a promotion became available in the department, Jeal 2 was again not selected as he did not have the required training, though he could have taken the training, and it would have been paid for by the company, he did not do so. Another candidate was then chosen. As a result, Jeal 2 became more difficult to work with and began to bad mouth John throughout the company as he searched for a new job within the company.

The difficult part about the first two examples is that are both situations within the church. We should not be having jealousy issues within the body of Christ, let alone in the same local church. We are all created differently with a different purpose and different talents, skills, gifts and resources. In the last example, the Jeal 2 character not only has a spirit of Jealousy, but also had narcissistic tendencies. So where do we go from here?

If you are struggling with a Spirit of Jealousy, even just slightly, you need to address it head on, and quickly. You do not want to allow it to take root and begin to stir up other areas that will only produce chaos in your life.

1. Admit it and don't try to justify it. It is wrong, it is telling God that what He has given you is not good enough. It opens the door to more evil.
2. Repent. Shut the door to evil, turnabout and seek the Lord for an understanding of how He sees you and all the wonder and beauty and talent He has provided in you. Yes, guys can be beautiful too!
3. Ask for Forgiveness. We should be doing this regularly anyway, but if we ask for forgiveness in this

area, we allow the Lord to open new doors for us, His doors. It will change your outlook.

4. Be Thankful. This is a feeling that may not happen right away, you must look at yourself and what you have with a new thankful heart. If you want more or an improvement in what you have, seek the Lord and have Him guide you in His ways. He will not give you an increase if you are not thankful for what you have at the present.

If you are in the position of having to deal with the Spirit of Jealousy from someone in your life, here are ways to evict the influence it is having over you.

1. Seek the Lord and pray over the situation. We want to make sure we are addressing the situation with an honest, earnest, open heart. We could be misreading or misinterpreting, and we want to allow for grace if we have made a mistake.
2. Pray for them. They are in a struggle, and your prayer could help them change.
3. Don't allow yourself to get upset by their behavior. The spirit of Jealousy is focused on creating chaos within that person but taking you down at the same time is only a bonus for them. Identify and separate the behavior from the person. This is much easier to say than to do, but your getting upset isn't helping you either.
4. Shift your position to cutoff opportunity or redirect attention. If, in the past, you have been willing to share personal information, hold back and instead ask them questions and allow them to talk about themselves. This could serve to let them know they

are heard and begin to quell feelings of insecurity or insignificance. Be genuine in this approach.

5. If the situation is just too toxic for you to be able to function at work, church or within the family, then you want to consider the process that is laid out for us in Matthew 18:15. Attempt to talk to your Jeal alone to address the issue. If that doesn't change, then take a witness or two to address the situation. If that still does not alleviate the issue, then add church leadership or an HR type person into the situation. I have only seen one church situation escalated past the leadership level.

People with a Spirit of Jealousy aren't usually going to continue down the road the same way once they have been confronted. They may switch tactics if there is no change but ask the Lord to reveal the truth in all circumstances and remain consistent in your behavior honoring to the Lord.

I hope you found that to be helpful for you or for someone you know. This spirit can be difficult to pinpoint and understand, but once you realize what kind of spirit you are dealing with, then you can almost anticipate what will come from them next. It's not a terribly creative spirit.

Chapter 13

Rejection

Next up is the Spirit of Rejection. I want to address how the Spirit of Rejection works to torment us and in contrast show how our best defense against rejection is forgiveness. We will also discuss signs to know if you are responding with a spirit of Rejection. We can then go on the offense by responding in love, which some believe is one of the most difficult acts we are asked to do as believers, but we'll see how it is truly simple.

Now, not all rejection is the Spirit of Rejection; let's be clear about that. But we have all been there. We have all experienced some sort of rejection in our lives. One part of rejection we don't acknowledge very often in our society today is that rejection does not always produce a negative outcome. How we process rejection is what determines our ability to handle challenge and establishes who we are in Christ as individuals in a healthy way. Not all rejection is created equal. When we are rejected as children by our family or in a marriage by our spouse, it can be much more traumatic than not being selected for a promotion. We need to recognize there is a distinction in rejection and not consider all rejection the same.

Let's examine a little bit about what Rejection is and how it works against us. Rejection is an inner wound that requires forgiveness for healing to begin. If we don't forgive, it allows the inner wound to begin to fester and infect the rest of our heart and mind. It will produce bitterness, anger, resentment and even hatred. Rejection can be traumatic. If we allow it to take root, rejection can produce lifelong sadness, depression, self-worth issues. The Spirit of Rejection is a tormenting demon. The only objective of Rejection is to bring you into bondage using your own pain against you. As an emotion, Rejection is frequently neglected, overlooked, hidden deep inside. There is usually a wound created from rejection that we don't want to deal with so we hide it. As a result, it becomes the root of many other issues we will deal with in our lives without realizing its original tie came out of a rejection. For some, the original act that produced the rejection is not even remembered, only the collateral damage that results. For others, the rejection is still raw and is like a recurrence over and over again.

When we are rejected, we feel overlooked, excluded, unloved, slighted, disrespected, undervalued, forgotten. The natural tendency when we are rejected is to defend ourselves which may result in lashing out, covering or shielding our heart, shutting out others. This may be an attempt to prevent being hurt again but even that response comes with a price because that self-isolation yields the same result as rejection - but you are instead choosing that for yourself. Self-rejection! You believe you can at least trust yourself, but you slowly begin to distrust others. Over time, this can develop into a paranoia if we allow it. You begin to question the smallest of things. Have you ever met someone who was paranoid?

I want to tell you about a man I worked with for a period of time who was seeking a deliverance. We will call him John. I try to call everyone Jane or John if you haven't picked up on that already. Anyhow, John was paranoid. In talking to John to better understand him I asked open ended questions to try to define his paranoia and find the strongman. I wanted to see where paranoia most exhibited itself. With John, anytime he spoke of the women in his life, he became more paranoid and made bold accusations against them. The accusations were not logical, and the more he spoke, the more we began to understand that he was "ghosted" numerous times which translates to "rejected" numerous times by these various women over a period of several years. The anger and hateful accusations made against these women were allowed to essentially percolate because the spirit of rejection had such a hold on John and deceived him into believing the odd accusations he made were true.

Rejection can deceive you into believing anything about yourself and about others. The idea is to keep you so wrapped up in this deceit, you can't focus on forgiving the person you believe has wronged you. Understand, I am not even saying here that in every situation we are being wronged; perception can be a lie as well. I can tell you with great certainty that John misread the intentions of some of the women he dated in the past and jumped to his own conclusions. When it didn't turn out the way he expected, he felt rejected. When he reacted poorly, he was "ghosted." We are all guilty of this at some level. How we respond is the key to defending our heart and mind. Let's look at some signs of the Spirit of Rejection at work in our lives:

Signs of Spirit of Rejection

·   The feeling no one understands you or accepts you

· Comparing yourself to others and in your mind, you are always less than others

· Feeling overlooked when you are not acknowledged for even small things, including situations where acknowledgement is not typically done

· Constantly seeking approval from others, sometimes going out of your way to be acknowledged, especially publicly

· Becoming angry, even bitter when you are not chosen, even if the person chosen was the better fit

· Becoming easily offended or defensive when being corrected, unable to handle being incorrect

· Thinking everyone is out to sabotage you

· Thinking you never fit in, so you become difficult to get along with

· Unwilling to forgive others whether they apologize for a wrong

· Believing you need to get back at everyone who "wrongs" you – unwillingness to forget

If you repeatedly see signs of this in your behavior, then we need to dig down and work on how to evict the Spirit of Rejection. Be honest with yourself. Only you know how you feel deep down. We want to root out Rejection so it doesn't have a chance to continue to grow and develop.

So how do we root it out? Forgiveness. This may require a look back to see where you may not have forgiven someone who wronged you and as a result created this attitude or behavior. If it's not you, maybe you see this in a family member or friend who struggles. This situation won't change until we learn how to forgive and defend our heart and mind the correct way.

Forgiveness is not easy. Forgiveness, depending on how deep the wound is, may even feel impossible. Let's look at how Jesus and Stephen handled pretty severe rejection with forgiveness.

Luke 23:34 shows us how Jesus forgave when he was rejected. This is the ultimate rejection. His own people were sacrificing him. They were rejecting Him as the Son of the God they claimed to worship. These men had written knowledge that Jesus would be coming, and they still rejected Him. They conspired to take His very life after trying to take everything else from Him first. I don't know anyone who has faced rejection at this level. Jesus continually faced rejection throughout His ministry, and He did not react sinfully. He never let Satan get a foothold in His life. He responded instead with forgiveness first and then love. It is important to understand that order because until we forgive, any attempt at love may not be genuine. I'm sure there are some people out there who can respond in love no matter what you do to them, but most of us are not that way. We must be honest with ourselves and our emotions so we can clear out what is preventing us from forgiveness and as a result, the full life Jesus promised in John 10:10. That was a promise - not a maybe it'll happen. God does not lie, God cannot lie; so if He says it is what He came to give to us, then it is ours to receive.

Another example is Stephen. He was able to forgive when he was rejected and stoned, Acts 7:59, *While they were stoning him, Stephen prayed, "Lord Jesus, receive my spirit." Then he fell on his knees and cried out, "Lord, do not hold this sin against them." When he had said this, he fell asleep.*

How many of us react this way? Stephen just gave a powerful, heartfelt, emotional and logical speech. It was a message that was true, undeniable and still the evil in those men's hearts blinded them to the truth, and they chose to take his life. Stephen was our first Christian martyr following Pentecost.

So, when we are rejected, or even if we feel rejected – meaning, if we are reacting in a way about something where nothing was intended toward us, or we misunderstand – getting to that place of forgiveness before we allow our heart and mind to become hurt is a rebuke in action. We are defending ourselves in that manner. Then when we can turn around and respond in love, going from defense to offense, spiritual warfare is taking place. We are denying the enemy access and evicting him from moving in our lives.

Let's walk through this together. First, we need to find a place in our hearts and minds to forgive who…everyone. We can't single anyone out, any offense out, we must let it all go and trust God to do what is best for us and for the other person. Think about it, have you ever offended someone, hurt them in a way they needed to forgive you? I know I have. What happens if they never forgave you? Is that what you want? What about all those people you don't even know you offended? Maybe there's more of those out there. Don't you want to be forgiven? So why hold back? True, we may be holding on to ill will over something done to us where the person who did it could care less, does that change your relationship with Jesus? Actually, yes. Matthew 6:14, *"For if you forgive other people when they sin against you, your heavenly Father will also forgive you"*

If Matthew 6:14 is true, and we know it is, then the opposite is true as well. If you don't forgive other people, then your heavenly Father will also not forgive you. Many of us know this is the case, but we get so caught up in the rightness or wrongness of the other person that we put ourselves in the position of not being forgiven for our own mistakes. Our doing so allows that demonic spirit the ability to give their root a nice firm place in our lives. Find out where you lack forgiveness and give it away. Then make it a point to forgive immediately as new offenses emerge.

Now that we have forgiveness under our belt, how can we move into a place of responding in love? Well, let's first examine love as Paul describes it in 1 Corinthians 13. I'm starting at verse 4, *"Love is patient, love is kind. It does not envy, it does not boast, it is not proud. It does not dishonor others, it is not self-seeking, it is not easily angered, it keeps no record of wrongs. Love does not delight in evil but rejoices with truth. It always protects, always trusts, always hopes, always perseveres. Love never fails."* Now when we look at love as Paul describes it, love doesn't seem overwhelmingly difficult to do after forgiveness. It doesn't say I have to go hug on anyone. It doesn't say I have to go to lunch with them; it doesn't say I have to invite them to my home and become besties. It simply says, when someone has rejected me in a way for me to be hurt, I need to first forgive them and then be patient and kind. I need to not be dishonoring, not be easily angered, not keep a record of wrongs, and not delight in evil, but rejoice in the truth. That is probably a huge run on sentence my mom, the English

135

teacher, would not like, but it's a true run on sentence. Don't make love more difficult than it is. Don't turn love into actions or behaviors it is not. Don't apply expectations to either forgiveness or love that are unrealistic and difficult to maintain. Once we start doing that to ourselves, we are creating our own challenges, and the enemy is right there to draw it out and torment us when our expectations are not met. Our love reaction comes from the heart, not the mind. The mind follows the heart. When our heart is right with the Lord and we forgive, our hearts are free to respond in love in so many ways we didn't realize were possible.

I say that in full confidence because I am not one who could be described as overly loving for all the years of my life. We moved a lot; my dad was in the military so every few years you started your life over again. I'm an introvert, so the majority of the time I dreaded moving and starting life over again and again. Having to start over did not serve to make me the most loving and open-hearted individual because anywhere you lived, you knew it was short lived. You lost friends. There was no internet, no social media back then so generally between their moves and your moves, you lost your friends. It could be lonely, sometimes you would be transferred with people you knew, and a familiar face was nice, but primarily I was on my own. So, for me, forgiveness isn't as much of an issue as the love aspect. Having children changed me for sure, but outside of that I struggled to "love" people as a whole. I had to step back and really examine my heart. When you have to find your new group of friends every move, there's a lot of rejection involved.

The hardest move was from Europe to Texas. We moved to a little town called Belton, and it was extremely difficult to make friends. Those kids knew each other almost since birth so someone coming in as a teenager, someone who dressed differently and acted differently, had a process to go through just to be accepted. Now I love Texas; ninety percent of my family is scattered throughout the state, but it was a struggle for me to when we made this move. I was torn apart by some of the girls because I was different. One day in particular I was wearing a pair of earrings I bought in Paris. I traveled all over Europe, and my wardrobe reflected that. You guys should have seen me in my Adam Ant years. I was a sight. Anyhow, someone asked me about the earrings, where I got them and I gave an honest response that I bought them in Paris without thinking anything of it because it wasn't unusual for me or my friends in Europe. That response, guys, that response traveled through so many girls, and I had no idea the reaction it would create. No one would say it to my face, which I found odd, but when I would pass or behind my back they would talk and make jokes, saying and I remember the words exactly to this day- as well as the posture and the outfit of the girl who said it "Yeah, Paris, more like Paris, Texas." I didn't even know there was a Paris Texas at that time, but that girl was known to be just mean, mean to girls she could bully. Not once did she ever approach me and say anything to me, she always the cowardly way. It irritated me for years. Close minded and cowardly people do irritate me, I have to be honest. I remember everything about it and that was like forty years ago. What I don't do though is care about it. I don't care that she treated me poorly, was rude, mean. I forgive her and all her friends. I respond in love, but notice it isn't hard at all to respond in love. I don't wish evil, I remember what happened, it is part of my history, but I don't keep a record of her offenses against me. I'm sure she did other things but even then, I knew she wasn't acting in good character, and I moved on in my life and forgot about her.

Sometimes acting in love doesn't require us to go overboard. I didn't need to go to her and say, "I forgive you for being a jerk to me for no reason and furthermore, I love you and I want to make sure you know how I feel." Just keep it simple. If you have multiple people to forgive, start with the easiest first and be sincere.

Chapter 14

Cursing

The Spirit of Cursing is a little different than some of the other demonic influences. I want to discuss how it works around us and comes at us through others. We also need to know how we should respond to these words being used against us. We need to understand spirits like Cursing will inhibit us in developing our time and relationship with the Lord. By developing our relationship with Him, we will rid ourselves of heavy burdens and demonic influences that have controlled us or limited us. We need to break chains so the Lord can release us for more.

The Lord offers us a way to get rid of demonic influences holding us back from our John 10:10 relationship with Him. The fullness He can provide. Whatever wounds we have, He can heal them. He is willing, He is able if we come to Him. The enemy created a divide with sin, but Jesus came to redeem us and as a result to provides us a bridge over that divide, so it no longer exists for us. The only thing He asks is that we take a step onto that bridge. That's it. He knows some of us will take one step, some will take ten, some will run up on it to meet him. He just asks us to take a step to meet Him. So, let's work some more on getting things out of our way so we can get ourselves to that bridge.

The conversation we are going to have about the Spirit of Cursing is not going to cover specific Curses. That's a separate discussion. This is not about using bad words -

those come out as a result of a number of issues and should change the closer we get to the Lord. What we are discussing is more about who this Spirit of Cursing is and how it functions.

The Spirit of Cursing is a strongman and a very loud spirit. Words are their weapon, and they use them very well to illicit pain. The Spirit of Cursing is very controlling. It uses fear tactics, manipulation, and plays on weakness to illicit the outcome it is seeking. Primarily, the outcome is division and instability. When believers are in one accord, miracles can happen, movements of the Holy Spirit can happen, but when we are divided and arguing amongst ourselves, we are unable to come together for the glory of God. Let's step back a minute and not even look at things from a believer's perspective. Look at our world. Look at all the issues we are having now that we were not having five years ago. Barely four years ago when we were all beginning to head into a lockdown we never saw coming, our countries, nearly every country in the world, was in a more stable place. Let me tell you more about the Spirit of Cursing, and then let's talk about who is having the greatest influence over our countries, our world, right now. This is not a political discussion; this is a Spiritual discussion.

The Spirit of Cursing uses Blasphemy, so insulting or lacking respect toward God. It goes deeper than that but at a high level that's what we are referring to here. There are Spirits who promote coarse jesting, which is the use of our words that cross a line of what we generally consider to be appropriate. Coarse jesting uses racist words, hateful words, and sexual innuendo to communicate. The Spirit of Cursing will use the Spirit of gossip, the Spirit of criticism, backbiting, the Spirit of mockery, belittling others as a tactic, and railing which is protesting or complaining angrily about something or someone. We don't use that term a lot, but I'm sure most of have experienced it at some point.

This Spirit of Cursing is a master at using words, words as a sharp blade, a weapon to tear apart everyone. Proverbs 12:18, *"The words of the reckless pierce like swords, but the tongue of the wise brings healing."* It doesn't matter who you are, what side you are on, the differences between us do not matter because the Spirit of Cursing does not care about our differences or our commonalities. This demonic spirit only cares about one thing and that is using words to tear each other apart. A demon has to create pain and chaos in our lives, that is their job and if they do not, they pay a price for that. Do you think that Satan is telling his demons, "Hey, guys, it's ok, you'll do better next time, just keep trying." No, it doesn't work like that. They are spirits of torment, and that is their job against us. There is no Christmas party coming up for them or a New Years celebration for a job well done this year. A demon's fate is no better than ours if we are lost in the world. So now let's talk about the world, our countries. Satan doesn't have favorites; there is no country that gets less attention. Even Iran, a country without Christianity for the most part is being torn apart by their own evil issues. Satan has no favorites he wants to spare from his wrath.

I want to make sure we understand how words work so well. Words instill fear. How many people are immobilized due to threats of violence? Violence everywhere has increased. Words turn into action. Our words matter. Our words carry power and authority. Our words produce results. Proverbs 18:21 tells us this, *"The tongue has the power of life and death, and those who love it will eat its fruit."* In this

141

proverb, tongue refers to our words but notice how it ends. In reference to fruit, it doesn't say those who love it will eat its good fruit. It says fruit. So, if you are spewing words of death and destruction, like we see in coarse jesting, gossiping, backbiting, railing all these demonic influences that associate with the Spirit of Cursing, then you can expect the fruit of death as a result.

Have you ever had someone say something to you that was rude or mean spirited? You knew they really meant it, and they were taking a stab at you but then they smiled and said, "Oh I was just joking" usually followed up by a "don't take things so serious" which is also improper grammar but that's not my point here. Well, do you know the Bible has a message for us about that very issue? Proverbs 26: 18-19, *"Like a maniac shooting flaming arrows of death is one who deceives their neighbor and says, 'I was only joking!'"* That behavior in the person behaving this way is likely demonically influenced if they are doing it repeatedly. In my experience when that behavior has been directed at me, it was motivated by a spirit of Jealousy. When you get the Spirit of Jealousy together with the spirit of Cursing, things will be said that are reckless in an attempt to bring one person down while giving the other, the offending party, a feeling of satisfaction that they were able to say the mean thing they wanted to say in a way they perceive to be socially acceptable.

Here is an example; it's a very subtle example of someone with a Spirit of Cursing against me, but it illustrates the point of how the spirits of jealousy and cursing work together. I had a corporate career from 1991 to 2023, and back in the 90's "business casual" was just coming into being so this occurred before there was a business casual. Now we are talking probably 1993 for this, it was before the Northridge earthquake in '94 and before my first child was born in '95. There was a group of about ten of us and every day, at about 10 am or so we always took a few minutes to head down to the lunchroom and get coffee, a snack or whatever and chit chat for a few minutes. On this particular day, I was wearing a dress, it was a pink dress, not hot pink, but professional bright conservative pink if there is such a thing. Anyhow, I was wearing heels, probably something pink because back then I was strict about needing everything to match head to toe. I've relaxed a bit these days, but anyhow a pink dress was what I was wearing on this day. There was a woman in the group; if you worked on the 5th floor you were welcome to join us. We didn't care if we knew you or not. The 5th floor was different than the rest of the building so 5th floor folks stayed together for the most part. Anyhow, Linda was her real name. I usually say Jane but this was almost thirty years ago so I feel confident no one will know who she is; anyhow, Linda seemed to not really care for me. I always assumed she had things going on in her life and was directing or misdirecting her jealousy or bitterness at me and on this day, she proved me right. She looked at me as she sat opposite me at the table and said, "I can't wait until you have children and your baby spits up all over your pretty dresses." Then she gave a little chuckle as if to say, just kidding. I looked at her, gave a moment to pause because I had to ask myself if she really just said that to me out loud, and then I just said, "Oh." Then I looked away and became a part of another conversation distancing myself from her from that moment forward. I never worried about her gossiping about me or about any backbiting. I didn't think anyone would join her in it, so I just never engaged with her afterwards. She showed me her character, and I didn't like it, and I wasn't going to be a part of whatever she was trying to do. How she chose to engage with people and the words she used were reckless, and as a result, people around her drifted away from her. Over time, she became withdrawn and isolated because she could not control her words. She spoke words of rudeness and negativity over people. Her lack of self-confidence and her lack of self-worth led her to use her words against others, and what was a normal weakness in most people, grew into something ugly in her. Our weaknesses are our vulnerabilities with these demonic influences. They know our weakness well because they feed off them to compound our problems.

Our response to someone who is using these demonic tactics against us intentionally is to be firm where firmness is called for and to dismiss those things that are not really aimed at us. Linda can feel about me however she wants, it doesn't affect me. Her words, mean spirited as they are, were a result of what was going on in her, not me. I could tell she was just weak and lashing out at me. So, her behavior, I dismissed and moved on with my life.

Let me give you a more recent example that illustrates being firm. This occurred a few years ago when we were in Turkey filming for our YouTube channel. On this particular day we were in Istanbul. We had a few hours of downtime, and we decided to spend a couple of hours walking to places I wanted to see but were not part of our filming itinerary. We were walking through a wide-open area near Istanbul University when we were approached by a man. We stopped to look something up in our phone, which is a tourist no- no, but unfortunately it was necessary. Being approached is nothing unusual, except that in this instance there were no shops anywhere near us. He used the usual tactics in trying to sell us something. This guy had books in English, history books and I love ancient history, especially as it relates to the

Bible, hence the YouTube Channel. Anyhow, Turkey was experiencing some financial challenges, as were many counties coming out of covid and trying to recover, so we were trying to buy only from people we liked if they had what we wanted. This guy, I instantly didn't like him at all, but I noticed the books he had were ones I hadn't seen elsewhere so I was somewhat interested in buying them and we began haggling over price. In Turkey, we were dealing in three currencies: the Turkish Lira, the Euro and the American dollar. This guy wanted Euro. We came to an agreement on price and as my husband was pulling out the cash he had in his pocket, he pulled out the wrong currency by mistake. Before he could correct himself, this guy, we'll call him Jerk instead of John, Jerk just went off on my husband with some very hateful, evil, belittling words that included a well stated and detail filled death curse of how he would become so sick he would be in the hospital before the end of day. It was the strangest encounter, and such an odd choice of words to say over seven Euro. I didn't initially care about this guy's behavior, his words, on the other hand, they for sure irritated me but what invoked a response from me was the curse. Immediately, I responded with an intensity and volume Jerk was not expecting from me. It escalated quickly between us, and I did rebuke him and let him know he had better get away from us. What he did was not tolerated by us, and we were not going to allow him to say those words over us in any way, shape or form. This was a risky move on my part but because as soon as the words of cursing over my husband's life came out, I understood why I didn't like this guy from the beginning, and I saw the demonic influence he was trying to use in the situation. Jerk's countenance changed, his posture shifted, and as he stepped in toward my husband, his eyes changed, and it happened in a split second when he saw the currency still coming out of my husband's pocket. I watched the currency coming out of his pocket as well and I was about to say, "those aren't the Euro" but didn't get to even speak because Jerk immediately tore into him with his verbal assault and curse. That is a situation where I would say be firm. Don't allow the enemy to have an opening, don't be nice and say sorry and allow those words to hang out there over your life. No! Rebuke it and make sure the one attacking you understands those words will not be allowed here and will have no power over you. Shut it down with your authority. Words matter. When the enemy uses words against us, our words are more powerful. Use the words from the Bible and come right back and tear him up with your sword, your scripture. Don't stop until the fight is over. There was a reason I reacted so strongly to these words. In 2019, my husband was in the hospital and because of complications, almost died from sepsis, with multiple surgeries. Then exactly one year later to the day, he was in the hospital again with another very serious infection and more surgery. We have concerns and must take care to avoid any type of relapse, especially when we travel. The words this guy used were specifically chosen, and there is no doubt in my mind it was the enemy attempting to speak a curse into what it thought was a weakness in us.

So how this encounter ended was with my husband trying to call me away while I was still verbally battling it out with this guy. I never used an inappropriate word. I used words the Lord provided. I will be completely transparent and explain that I was not happy with my husband trying to pull me back and afterwards I asked him next time, let me stand. I will never back down in a spiritual fight like that. His concern, of course, was we were in a country not particularly favorable to Americans at times, and we were loud - we were very loud. At no time did I feel I was in danger; I knew where I was, who I was, what I was doing and why I was doing it. Within moments of my stepping away, I turned around to make sure Jerk stayed back, and that man was nowhere to be found. He literally disappeared, and we were in a wide-open space. It would have taken him a few minutes to walk through the wide-open, mostly empty, space we were in. We were in the center, but he was just gone. I believe, and you do not have to believe with me, but I know what I saw in that man; I believe he was a demonic entity. He had just the type of product to sell that would enable him to engage us in a dialogue. I actually wanted the books he had, they were not anywhere else in my travels, and I always look at the books when we go to a site. Anyhow, the location of this guy selling to us was odd. I generally dismiss people selling to me on the street when we travel. It is constant, and you must be careful of who you are interacting with in those moments as you may be set up for something else while you are distracted. This guy wasn't on the street; it wasn't an area where street vendors were located because it wasn't an area where tourists would go. His behavior, demeanor, and the changes I saw manifest were abnormal. Our weakness was in being concerned about a relapse and having to go to a Turkish hospital. The specificity of the curse he used was too convenient to be coincidence, followed by his disappearance afterward. Literally only seconds had passed when I turned back to look for him, and all I saw the woman feeding the pigeons as before, and the sparse number of businesspeople walking as before. It was early in the morning, but as I spun around in the circle, he was nowhere.

These type of encounters happen every day. We need to recognize and take seriously the words that are spoken over us, even by ourselves. Don't say anything over yourself that is negative or invites or allows the enemy to operate in that negative word over you. Our words matter. If you are in a situation where responding like I did in Istanbul is not appropriate, which in reality is probably most situations, the words spoken over you can still be rebuked. You can use scripture to counterattack without the other person even hearing it. You are not speaking to the person, it's the demon influencing the person, so you can whisper it, you can mouth it, just address it. Don't let the enemy speak over you without you shutting it down. Use the authority we have been given.

What if this is going on, or you think it is, but it's not to your face or you just aren't sure? What if you are dealing with this from a family member or someone from work where you must be around them consistently? What if you have no support? I hear this a lot, and it can feel very defeating. Here is how you can handle it and know that the Lord is going to intervene.

1.   Ask the Lord to reveal the truth in the situation. We want to bring the dark to the light.

2.   Ask the Lord if there is anything that you have done that has allowed the enemy to work in your life.

        a.   Repent and ask for forgiveness if the Lord reveals anything to you

        b.   Rebuke the enemy and use your scriptures

        c.   Pray quietly whenever you are in the presence of the person with whom you are having the issue

3.   Set aside time each day with your scriptures to pray and seek wisdom for how to proceed if this is ongoing until the Lord guides you to resolution. Document prayers and answered prayers for testimony and to build your faith.

Jesus continually had to battle against the Spirit of Cursing by the Pharisees while He traveled throughout His ministry, and to a lesser degree by the Sadducees, while He was in Jerusalem. They continually blasphemed against Him. They criticized Him, plotted against Him, mocked Him railed at Him, spread lies to anger the crowd and tried to trap Him and trick Him into saying or doing the wrong thing. Jesus stood His ground and was firm. He knew the Word and He used it.

In Matthew 12, the Pharisees accused Jesus of being in cohorts with Satan. He responded and His final words to them on that subject is this in verse 36, *"But I tell you that everyone will have to give account on the day of judgment for every empty word they have spoken. For by your words you will be acquitted, and by your words you will be condemned."*

Know that Jesus knows what we say and what is being said to us. Trust Him to help you through a situation and take a step on that bridge.

Chapter 15

Accusation

The Spirit of Accusation. This is a big one, and I know there are people out there struggling with this and don't even realize it's a demonic spirit demonizing them.

The Spirit of Accusation is an incredibly ugly, ugly spirit. It works as both a quiet spirit at times as it leads us to attack ourselves and a loud spirit as it leads us to attack others. Let's dig a little deeper into who this Spirit of Accusation is and what they are about.

The Spirit of Accusation is a Stronghold demon. Accusation is a Spirit of the antichrist; it is a very powerful demonic spirit. Typically, you will find the Spirit of Judgment, the Spirit of Criticism and the Spirit of Faultfinding associated with Accusation. Remember, there are a lot of associations, so you could find bitterness working to gain hold; Strife could appear due to Judgment, Criticism or Faultfinding. There are frequently also Religious spirits that will worm their way in to create conflicts.

Let's talk a bit about why the Spirit of Accusation is such a powerful Spirit. First, one of the names the Bible uses to describe and name Satan is that of our Accuser. One place we find this is Revelation 12:10, "*Then I heard a loud voice in heaven say: Now have come the salvation and the power and the kingdom of our God, and the authority of his Messiah. For the accuser of our brothers and sisters, who accuses them before our God day and night, has been hurled down."* This event is in the future, so during the past, which is part of our present, the passage describes the accuser going before God day and night against us. The Accuser has invested a great deal of time in coming against us, so we need to understand how that impacts us and use discernment to rebuke it when it is happening.

Second, we need to understand that the Spirit of Accusation is a legalistic spirit. What does that mean exactly? Well, a legalistic spirit wants to look for the wrong in others to then present judgment or condemnation. The Spirit of Accusation will often use guilt or shame to get to us and bring us down. As a believer, the Spirit of Accusation will bring up our past sins, our old life and our failures to bring us to a place of condemnation. The reason the Spirit wants to do this is to convince us that our past sins remain and cause us to doubt that our sins have already been forgiven by the blood of Jesus. There are so many, too many, Christians who have accepted Jesus as their Savior but are still carrying their sins - carrying a burden they were never asked to carry. He died for us so that those sins would no longer be a part of our lives. If we allow the Spirit of Accusation to gain a foothold in our lives with this thinking, then we are telling Jesus that what He did for us is not good enough.

Where Christians get confused is in understanding the difference between condemnation from the Accuser and conviction from the Holy Spirit. They are two entirely different events. Condemnation places our sin burden back on us. Condemnation tells us we must do something to earn our forgiveness with works or acts to make amends for our sins. It saddles us with tasks that are meant to get us to focus on the tasks or the sins. It heavily uses guilt and shame to tear us down and manipulate us to believe we are still not worthy. In doing this, it creates a chasm in our relationship with the Lord. It will also then take those feelings and turn them on others. By using finger pointing techniques, and accusing others to not only bring you down, but anyone you can criticize, judge or find fault with, whether it is true or not.

The Holy Spirit works entirely differently in us. The Holy Spirit uses conviction in our hearts to lead us from our sinful life, no matter how big or small, to Him. He uses His right and true ways to lead us to repentance and back in relationship with him. He does not accuse, that is not His way. He encourages and uses His loving ways to guide us on the right path. Paul tells us in 2 Timothy 3:16, *"All Scripture is God-breathed and is useful for teaching, rebuking, correcting and training in righteousness, so that the servant of God may be thoroughly equipped for every good work."* Proverbs 3:6 tells us, *"In all your ways submit to Him and He will make your paths straight."* The Bible is full of direction from the Lord that will lead us to success in Him. Think of it the way Proverbs 24:3 describes it, *"By wisdom a house is built, and through understanding it is established; through knowledge its rooms are filled with rare and beautiful treasures."* We can't get that through condemnation of the enemy; we need to recognize condemnation versus conviction and correction.

Think about Job, he was an upright man, but the accuser was allowed to continually demonize him. He tried several tactics, but Job remained strong, not perfect, but how many of us would? I can tell you I don't know if I would come close to maintaining the composure and faith of Job if I were in his position, but he remained steadfast to the Lord. If you haven't read the book of Job, it's a good read; it's long. Know that going into it, but it's a good read.

153

Think about Joseph, he was wrongly accused of sleeping with or attempting to sleep with Potiphar's wife, and was wrongly imprisoned, and that's after being sold into slavery by his brothers. He, too, remained steadfast and rebuked the attempts of the enemy to accuse him and take him into judgment against God or his brothers, or into bitterness against the chief cupbearer for forgetting Joseph and leaving him in jail. Those stories are in Genesis 39 and 40.

Here is what Jesus had to say when speaking to the Pharisees - a legalistic religious group in his day - in describing the Accuser in John 8:44, "*You belong to your father, the devil, and you want to carry out your father's desires. He was a murderer from the beginning, not holding to the truth, for there is no truth in him. When he lies, he speaks his native tongue, for he is a liar and the father of lies.*"

A few weeks ago, a friend of mine, we'll call him John, was in a conversation with someone that he trusted. Both men are believers. In the conversation, John's well-meaning friend told him he thinks John is carrying around guilt and shame from something in his past. John considered this friend someone he trusted, so he couldn't think of any guilt or shame he was feeling but said he would pray about it. John spent 3 days, praying, asking the Lord, asking those close to him if he has ever alluded to or spoken of anything where he exhibited guilt or shame. John came up empty handed and was a little frustrated. John again went back to the Lord and wanted to know why the Lord wouldn't just let him know if this was an issue; he would gladly have dealt with it immediately if he had known it was an issue. He kept asking the Lord, "What is it, Lord? I just can't find anything in my heart that feels this guilt or shame." John knew he wasn't perfect, but he had done a lot to change his life. He also knew that just thirty-six hours before this comment was made to him that he had been helping someone else let go of their past and remind them the cross took all of that away. That was how John lived his life. On day five, John finally settled down enough to actually hear what the Lord had to say to him in response to his questioning and it was this: "The words I gave to your friend were meant to be an encouragement to you. They were presented to you not as I intended, but based on what was in his heart, not yours. It's ok, don't let it change your relationship with your friend."

John's situation is unusual and unfortunate. Sometimes we say something to one another with the best intentions, not realizing we might be being used as a tool of the enemy to accuse us of things and even couch them directed toward our Christian friends. These are all tactics, ways the enemy will use to tear us down and get us to question who we are in Christ and how God sees us. John's friend meant zero harm. John knows that, but the enemy could have used this situation to trap John into getting upset with his friend as well. John didn't let that happen and understands that sometimes, even with the best intentions, people don't always get it right.

If you have someone gossiping about you, saying things to try to destroy your credibility, or blaming you continually for things you truly are not responsible for, then you are likely dealing with a Spirit of Accusation coming against you. On the other hand, if you find that you are the one criticizing, making accusations that are false, gossiping, keeping a record of wrongs, then you likely are being demonized and are enabling the Spirit of Accusation to use you and work through you to tear down others. If you are allowing yourself to be used, you will need to take responsibility for it.

155

How do you take responsibility for your behavior and then change your behavior? I'm glad you asked. Here are 6 Steps to Evict the Accuser:

1.   Acknowledge it: Identify if what you are feeling is condemnation or conviction. Confirm if what is being said is true or a false accusation. We must be honest with ourselves here if we have a sin issue. This is also the point where we need to decide and take a stand if it is false, we don't accept the lie as a truth.

2.   Understand it: Identify condemnation tactics and why they were used. Have they worked in the past? If we are feeling convicted, make sure we understand biblically why we are having sin issues needing to be addressed.

3.   Accept conviction and correction: This is what we need from the Lord, so don't turn away, turn toward God even if we don't like it. His way is always the best way.

4.   Repent: Break ties, rebuke the enemy and prepare for the enemy to come back and attempt to demonize you again. They are waiting for you to be worn down and become weak. We want to rebuke in situations of both false accusations and in any attempts to tempt us back into the sin we were participating in when we experienced conviction from the Holy Spirit. In both situations, we want to evict the enemy.

        a.   False Accusation: Rebuke the enemy for false accusations – name them (gossip, bitterness, jealousy, criticism)

  b. Sin Conviction: Rebuke the enemies associated with your sin issues – name them. (addiction, jealousy, gossip)

5. Seek Forgiveness: Release it to the Lord: Take whatever occurred, whatever is triggering you, hand it over to Him and let go of it. This means forgiving yourself as well. Some people really struggle with this and that is telling the Lord His forgiveness isn't enough. Hand it over and let go of it.

6. Replace it: We want to ask the Lord to reveal the truth in all situations. Invite the Holy Spirit into the situation. If we are going to evict the enemy and his influence, we need to replace accusation and fill ourselves with what the Holy Spirit provides. Use your scriptures; here are two that reveal the role of the Holy Spirit in our lives.

John 15:26, *"When the Advocate comes, whom I will send to you from the Father—the Spirit of **truth** who goes out from the Father—he will testify about me."*

John 16:13, *"But when he, the Spirit of **truth**, comes, he will guide you into all the **truth**. He will not speak on his own; he will speak only what he hears, and he will tell you what is yet to come."*

If you are struggling with replacing it, go back and check if you completed all the steps. If we are in a situation that has been going on for years, it may take us time to walk through all these steps and have it all completed. If we don't do it sincerely and with our heart and mind on the same page, we will likely be encountered with the situation multiple times until we complete it all in its entirety. The Accuser isn't wanting to make it easy for you. Seek the Lord and remain steadfast in evicting the Accuser's influence in your life.

Chapter 16

Bitterness

Demons in my mind fall into one of two categories, quiet or loud. What I mean by this is how a person reacts to being demonized can be heard as the demonic spirit begins to work through the person. People who have what I consider to be quiet spirits will generally keep to themselves about it. For example, loneliness, guilt and doubt tend to keep the person hurting more inwardly. By being quiet about it, they don't often seek help or reach out to others but instead suffer quietly. Other spirits I consider loud, and Bitterness is a loud spirit. When someone is bitter you hear it through their words. You will see it in their actions, rolling their eyes, stares, piercing looks, interrupting, sighs when you speak. You also see and hear it in how they treat others. A bitter person is often rude, sarcastic, vindictive, creates obstacles, difficult to work with and creates issues when there is no need for issues. They want to win in a situation, and if it can bring you down as a result, all the better. As the Spirit of Bitterness grows, anger and hatred manifest in more vocal ways. It creates fear in others and can push people away because they don't want to hear it or deal with it, which then again feeds the spirit of Bitterness in that person.

What is the Spirit of Bitterness? how does it function and what influences generally are associated with it? The Spirit of Bitterness is frequently a strongman. It typically develops early in us as a result of an experience where we feel we have been wronged, cheated or betrayed. There is a deep emotional tie to our heart and whatever it is that has occurred to us. Often there is aggression because the reaction is that something was "done" to us. The emotional tie between the negative experience and our heart is so damaged, we are unable to overcome the hurt and resentment gets a foothold in our lives. Now in reality, our inability to overcome hurt so resentment is a lie the enemy is telling us, so there is also a Spirit of Deception involved. If we don't identify the lie, we are being told we are not able to overcome being hurt nor able to turn to the Lord. The belief in the lie can then allow a root to develop in our heart and our mind that is very difficult to cut out. Unforgiveness and hatred move in, and they can function slowly and creep their way through our heart without us realizing how deep the roots are forming. Over time it shapes our behaviors, reactions to others, our activities, our outlook and through these areas other influences are allowed to enter our heart as well. Typically, with the Spirit of Bitterness, you will find the companions of resentment, hatred, temper, anger, retaliation, unforgiveness, and all of these can then escalate to violence and, unfortunately in extreme cases, murder.

Let's see what the Bible tells us about the spirit of bitterness. We have several scriptures here, and I want to look at them and identify what they say about us, our hearts, our minds, and where they tell us it is going to take us.

Hebrews 12:15 warns us in this way, "*See to it that no one falls short of the grace of God and that no bitter root grows up to cause trouble and defile many.*" The result of falling short of the grace of God, not allowing God to redeem you, not entering into that relationship, allows a bitter root to grow. What is the result? Who does it affect? Everyone around you!

160

Deuteronomy 29:18, "*Make sure there is no man or woman, clan or tribe among you today whose heart turns away from the Lord our God to go and worship the gods of those nations; make sure there is no root among you that produces such bitter poison.*" Speaks to relationship and bitterness associated with poison.

Deuteronomy 32:32, "*Their vine comes from the vine of Sodom and from the fields of Gomorrah. Their grapes are filled with poison, and their clusters with bitterness.*" This is an analogy. What happened to Sodom and Gomorrah? God's judgment left nothing to spare.

1 Samuel 30:6, "*David was greatly distressed because the men were talking of stoning him; each one was bitter in spirit because of his sons and daughters. But David found strength in the Lord his God.*" Bitterness leading to hatred, violence, murder

Proverbs 14:10, "*Each heart knows its own bitterness, and no one else can share its joy.*" Again, discussing bitterness in the heart and who does it hurt? Everyone!

Jeremiah 2:19, "*Your wickedness will punish you; your backsliding will rebuke you. Consider then and realize how evil and bitter it is for you when you forsake the Lord your God and have no awe of me,*" *declares the Lord, the Lord Almighty.*" These are the Lord's words through the prophet Jeremiah, and see how the Lord associates evil and bitterness together? This shows there is no future in bitterness.

Amos 5:7, "*There are those who turn justice into bitterness and cast righteousness to the ground.*" This is an amazing scripture that reveals the two sides - justice vs bitterness and in casting righteousness to the ground, bitterness brings that to fruition, it is the opposite of righteousness.

Amos 6:12, *"Do horses run on the rocky crags? Does one plow the sea with oxen? But you have turned justice into poison and the fruit of righteousness into bitterness—"* Again showing the two things that do not belong together. Depicting bitterness as the opposite of righteousness.

Acts 8:23, *"For I see that you are full of bitterness and captive to sin."* Here bitterness is now associated with sin. We need to be real with ourselves if we have bitterness; it's sinful and if you are unclear about that, we'll get into why here shortly.

Romans 3:14, *"Their mouths are full of cursing and bitterness."* Cursing is one of our other demons to address during this series and again see the association Paul is making with bitterness. We don't want this in our mouths, our hearts, our minds, or our lives anywhere.

James 3:14, *"But if you harbor bitter envy and selfish ambition in your hearts, do not boast about it or deny the truth."* This is another way of saying what we call nowadays, be transparent or authentic. It really speaks to being honest with ourselves and with others.

We have identified what the spirit of bitterness is, and we have looked at several verses that give an equally damning depiction of what bitterness will do in our lives. So how do we get rid of it?

Well first, we need to acknowledge it.

If we have a Spirit of Bitterness, don't try hide it, it will find its way out whether we like it or not. It will be apparent in our words, attitudes, behaviors; it will not be silent. Address it head on and understand the reasons behind why the Spirit of Bitterness was able to creep into your heart. We want to close any doors we have open or past hurts that will cause a closed door to reopen. The Spirit of Bitterness knows our weaknesses, so we need to call on the strength of the Lord.

Now maybe you don't have a full-blown case of bitterness, and so you are feeling pretty good right now. Well, what about a baby case of bitterness that doesn't rear its head very often, so you don't even remember you have an issue with someone or something? When you don't see people regularly, it's easy to forget an old hurt. It's easy to be reminded of a childhood resentment. Ask the Holy Spirit to jog your mind so you can find any old bitterness and get yourself ready to root it out. This is not an easy task for some, so if you can, pray for those who are reading this as you are and who may be dealing with bitterness as a result of a traumatic event or a betrayal. Carrying old hurts around is heavy and drains us of life. The Lord is available and wants to heal deep wounds, but He cannot do that if we are not willing to let Him do it and release it to Him. I am asking you to truthfully do the work to investigate your heart, identify any bitterness, resentment, unforgiveness, violence, temper, anger, retaliation, and even murder and that includes thoughts of murder.

What if you were someone who was abused, mistreated or neglected in some way as a child, and the person responsible for that has passed away? The fact that they have passed away does not negate your need to address it and clear out any spirit of bitterness. You may have been trespassed in an incredibly evil way or neglected. I certainly wish I could take it away and you never had to experience it, but I can't. Jesus, however, can help you overcome it. I know some of us will have some very real deep hurts, but we need to allow Jesus to take that on for us and begin that healing process so we can be free of old pain.

So secondly, after we acknowledge it, we need to be willing to release it to the Lord. We must let go of any bitterness, resentment - all of those demonic influences. Releasing is not an easy step. We are making ourselves extremely vulnerable and that is a scary, uncomfortable place to be, but we must be willing to have the courage to do that because remember, the Lord will replace it with His love and His compassion for you. When you are going through the process to release it, it requires your heart and mind to work together. You can say in your mind you are releasing it, but if you are still carrying it in your heart, then you haven't released it. It may take some time to get your heart and mind to work together, but it is possible. For some, it also helps to get their body involved. If this is you, once you have done all the work and are ready to release it to the Lord, then create some physical activity that demonstrates a release. For some it's writing a letter to the Lord, for some it's letting out a good cry, for some it's letting out a good scream. Whatever fits for you, do that and don't look back.

The third step we want to make in this process is incredibly important. You can do all the work but if you fail to do step three, then you will likely find yourself right back where you started at some point. Anytime we evict demonic influences, we need to go back and fill that void with what we receive from the Lord. Paul tells it to us this way: Ephesians 4:31-32, *"Get rid of all bitterness, rage and anger, brawling and slander, along with every form of malice. Be kind and compassionate to one another, forgiving each other, just as in Christ God forgave you."*

Forgiveness. If you are willing to release it to the Lord, the way you support that release is to forgive whoever was involved in the Spirit of Bitterness coming to fruition in your heart. Now let's say you have read along this far and you have found no deep bitterness, but what about pre-bitterness? You have some feelings. You have not allowed bitterness to take root but it is certainly working to try to do just that. Forgiveness.

To overcome and evict the enemy, we need to remember who Jesus is and ask for His light to drive out the darkness of bitterness. Now let's take this another step further. What if we have done something that creates bitterness in someone else?

I want to share with you one of my own experiences. I have a blended family. So, I have been divorced, and as I was in the beginning stages of the divorce, I was dealing with a lot at one time. It had been a really, really ugly situation for four years until we had agreement that a divorce was happening. Once I had biblical grounds, everything began to move forward. I had four young children at the time. I had a lot to figure out. I gave up the house to reduce the number of contestable things so now I needed to find a new place to live, and we all were going to have new schedules. All the usual life activities of four kids had to be rearranged. When a friend of mine heard that I was getting divorced, she reached out to me. We weren't terribly close, but she reached out to me because she was recently divorced as well. Her situation was similar to mine so I think in me she saw someone who would be willing to commiserate. I wasn't terribly comfortable about discussing details of my situation, so I mostly listened. Within a few minutes I could tell the conversation was clearly going down the path of men bashing. While I understood her position, I felt it wasn't healthy for me nor necessary at this point in my life. I knew I was out of an awful situation; I would be safe. My kids would no longer be in that environment, and I needed to remain focused on what I needed to accomplish for this transition. I knew developing a relationship with this person in her current state would be toxic for me, and I just couldn't do it. I then had to explain to her I couldn't do it. I needed her to understand it wasn't helpful to me in my situation. In doing that, I immediately created a divide between me and this woman that lasted for years. She wouldn't talk to me; even when she saw me, she seemed to loathe me. As years passed, I could tell she had become bitter toward me. I could see she was bitter towards several people, and it was hard to watch, but she would not listen to anyone about making changes. I didn't see her for 15 years and then a mutual friend called and shared with me that this woman was sick. It was serious, and I wasn't sure what I wanted to do about it. She had refused to talk to me the last time I saw her, and behaved pretty obnoxiously toward me, but after a few months I decided to call, and we talked. We never spoke of the break in the relationship, and instead we just shared our lives. I felt good about it. I never want to be the cause nor contribute to the cause of anyone else feeling bitterness. Whether you are right or wrong, knowing someone is hurting from an experience with you is not what we need. Even though I know I made the right choice at the time, I should have followed up sooner or tried to explain myself better. My friend passed away four months after I decided to make that call. We spoke a few more times in those last months but knowing she passed free of the bitterness, helped me to forgive myself of what I thought I could have done better. Never forget, forgiveness also applies to ourselves.

If you are dealing with a spirit of Bitterness, chances are, those around you know it. Those around you have seen it, heard it, been the recipient of it and may have chosen to step back from you as a result. Check your heart and mind and let the Lord replace it with His love for you.

Chapter 17

Insecurity

In Chapter 16, we talked about quiet spirits and loud spirits. I explained that people who have what I consider to be quiet spirits will generally keep to themselves about it. For example, loneliness, guilt and doubt tend to keep the person hurting more inwardly. By being quiet about it, they don't often seek help or reach out to others but instead suffer quietly. The Spirit of Insecurity is what I would consider a quiet spirit. Most of us experience insecurity in some area at some level. We generally don't share that feeling of insecurity with others. We keep it to ourselves, sometimes deep inside, and keeping it inside is what can allows it to grow and mutate.

Our insecurities can also trigger temptations that produce bad fruit if we allow the temptations to develop to fruition, no pun intended. Once we have acted on our temptations, we may be able to hide it for a while, but sooner or later, if what we have done has produced bad fruit we will not be able to hide it for long. We can try to cover it up; we can attempt to blame others, and find ways to justify, but ultimately the Holy Spirit cannot be manipulated. We will need to acknowledge there are consequences for our bad choices and be honest about when we lack self-control versus when we are being demonized. In both cases, we need to be responsible for evicting the enemy when we are being demonized as well as for developing self-control. This becomes more challenging when we are keeping our insecurities to ourselves versus seeking support. Let's dig deeper into the Spirit of Insecurity so we can understand how he operates and who he operates with against us.

The Spirit of Insecurity is a strongman demon. You will likely see the Spirit of Inferiority, self-pity, the spirit of loneliness, timidity, the spirit of shyness, inadequacy and the spirit of ineptness working together with Insecurity. Once the Spirit of Insecurity has a foothold, the Spirit of Accusation can easily begin to operate as well. This will also allow the Spirit of Cursing to easily maneuver its way into our lives if we don't recognize it working to influence us. Sounds overwhelming, doesn't it? By working together as an orchestra, these demonic spirits have had centuries upon centuries of experience in manipulation. If we don't have a relationship with the Holy Spirit and make that relationship a priority, you may never see this coming.

I want to take a minute and discuss something I think is important to circle back on because I haven't discussed it in a while. We don't ever want to live our lives thinking there is a demon around every corner or that demons are responsible for every bad thing in our life or to give excuses for our behavior. We cannot, under any circumstances, say a demon is responsible and thereby rid ourselves of any responsibility. I talk about these demons or spirits and explain who they will associate with so we can discern - not excuse. Demonization is real, and I want to respect the difference between demonization and our lack of self-control or (un)willingness to maintain control. I hope that makes sense because we never want to be about excuses.

Ok, back to Insecurity. We are going to go through some real examples of people dealing with Insecurity and how it has entangled their lives and then reveal what the Bible tells us about it.

I want to share with you a conversation recently that really, really bothered me. The reason I am sharing it with you is because I want you to be aware that there are people out there claiming to be Christian yet and saying things like this that lead others astray. We need to know that this sort of heresy, blasphemy, lie, evil, misguided, lost and incredibly stupid theology exists; yes, I said stupid. Even though I have a chance to change it before you read this, I am not going to change it. Here is a real-life example: A new believer, who was struggling, asked for evidence supporting the existence of Christ and Christianity as a whole. Now I say new believer only because that is what he called himself. In my opinion, you cannot ask that question and be a believer at the same time. You either believe Christ existed and died for your sins or that He did not. It is black or white - no gray here. He was insecure in his belief and knowledge of who Jesus is and who Jesus is in his life. His question reveals to me a lack of understanding but even more about what he is going to need once he develops a relationship with Jesus, if he wants to stand strong. Asking for evidence of the very existence of Jesus and even further for Christianity, which has been documented for 2000 years now is exactly what this demon wants to do. Having you question everything concerning Jesus and everything that has occurred since His crucifixion and resurrection breeds insecurity. If Jesus didn't exist, He can't be your Savior. While I am happy that this guy was reaching out and asking for help, it brings to mind the parable Jesus gave us in Matthew 13 about the seed falling on rocky ground and dying out soon. This may sound like an extreme example, but it's more common than you may realize. Now let me tell you about the answer he received, and I hope you find it as scary as I did coming from someone who is also claiming to be Christian. This is the response…remember the question was asking for evidence supporting the existence of Christ and Christianity.

The answer given was this: This new believer was guided to instead of looking for this evidence of Christ's existence, he should develop his relationship with God. I agree with that in part, except the question was about Jesus; and if I were to be more specific, it's a relationship with Jesus as our Savior that we need to have in place as our savior. Jesus tells us in John 14:6, *"I am the way and the truth and the life. No one comes to the Father except through me."* Let me get to the part of the statement that I thought I misunderstood when it was first said, "we must establish our relationship with the Holy Spirit and not take the Bible as God's word but simply a book about God. This guy went on to call it an important book, but it is not holy, not perfect and using it as a replacement for your relationship with God and the good sense God gave you is idolatry." That, my friends, is an entirely demonic response given to a new believer who does not know better. That is Satan from the beginning to the end because it is designed to take us away from the Word. If we do not know the Word, we will forever be influenced by Satan to draw us away. This is what God has to say about His Word. *"In the beginning was the Word and the Word was with God and the Word was God."* That's John 1:1.

What would you do if you asked a question or heard someone ask the question and someone gave a response similar to the one above? I would say, "I rebuke that, it is not the truth," and then quote the correct scripture. You don't have to be a Bible scholar. Jesus isn't asking us to know every detail and recite it as if we have memorized the entire Bible;

don't get intimidated by the Bible. You just have to read so you know: Hey, what that guy said isn't right. Then go find the truth in the Bible. Ask a pastor. That is how we equip ourselves to know when the enemy is coming at us with lies. That is also how we defeat our own insecurities in our of lack of knowledge. Jesus always responded to Satan with the correct use of scripture, and so should we.

We went on a slight tangent from where I was wanting to go, so let's get back on track. I want to tell you about a woman who reached out to me for help, we will call her Jane. Jane is in her 40's, never married, though she would like to be, and she is lonely. She does not have a stable income, or a stable home situation and is unable to maintain a job. Jane is demonized by the Spirit of Insecurity joined by inadequacy, ineptness and inferiority. There are others as well not a part of the Insecurity strongman, but Insecurity is the one who controls a lot of what she does. She has a serious issue with self-pity, and to be completely transparent, has a victim mentality because she is unable to admit her faults. She has a lot of loneliness because she seeks her security in relationships with men, but they are not healthy relationships. They are primarily sexually driven so they don't last long, and she is not valued by these men. Her self-worth is then affected. She is in a cycle she has been unable to get out of on her own. There are not a lot of people out there who are demonized at Jane's level. She is on the extreme end of the spectrum, but she gives us a clear picture of what can happen when it gets out of control. Ultimately, Jane must be willing to work on the root causes that drive her behaviors and reactions. Jane is a deliverance case and in the time I have spent with her, we have been able to clear out lower level demons, but Jane has not yet been able to completely evict all her demonic influences. Jane has a long road ahead of her because as soon as we are able to evict one demon, she decides to fill the void with something else that is not of the Lord. That is what brings her comfort, and she only trusts what she knows. Insecurity is a lack of trust, a lack of confidence. The one thing in our lives we know we can count on is Jesus. Without the ability to trust in Jesus, we will not be able to grow. James tells it to us this way in James 1:6, *"But let him ask in faith, with no doubting, for the one who doubts is like a wave of the sea that is driven and tossed by the wind."*

One of my favorite scriptures I keep in my scripture journal is Jeremiah 17:7-8, *"But blessed is the one who trusts in the Lord, whose confidence is in him. They will be like a tree planted by the water that sends out its roots by the stream. It does not fear when heat comes; its leaves are always green. It has no worries in a year of drought and never fails to bear fruit."*

One of the best things you can do to rid yourself of Insecurity is to read the Bible. As you read, you begin to know who God is, to see the coming of Jesus, to understand Jesus and to understand the truth of our lives in Him. You will know why you feel the way you do about decisions you make and will be less influenced by anything that is not God's plan for your life. That is Security in Him.

How do we go from experiencing Insecurity to Security in Him. Well, I have our 5 steps to Security in Him:

1. Acknowledge it: We have to be able to admit our insecurities and be willing to step outside of our comfort zone to change and develop. Make a list of all the areas where you know the Spirit of Insecurity has impacted your life.

2. Understand it: Identify our insecurities and why we have them. What are our triggers? Do not accept the enemy lies as truth.

3. Repent: Rebuke the enemy and seek the Lord for guidance. Find a scripture to stand on for your rebuke such as Proverbs 3:5-6, *"Trust in the Lord with all your heart and lean not on your own understanding; in all your ways acknowledge him and he will make your paths straight."* That scripture is relatively easy to remember, but it speaks volumes as to your intentions and how you plan to anchor your life moving forward. The enemy already knows the scripture is true; by saying it in your rebuke, you are letting the enemy know you know it too.

4. Replace it: Our security comes from the Lord. We need to take all the areas the enemy previously occupied and submit them to the Lord. We want to ask the Lord to reveal the truth in all situations. Invite the Holy Spirit into the situation. If we are going to evict the enemy and his influence, we need to replace insecurity and fill ourselves with the truth and trust in what the Holy Spirit provides.

5. Be accountable: This step is important because Insecurity will quietly come back and try to pull you into being shy about your struggle. Find someone you can lean on to help you as you build and develop in strength. Meet with that person regularly. Make a plan to develop yourself in all those areas you know you have insecurities. Refer to the list you made in step 1. Tackle one at a time if it's a long list. Make it manageable.

Chapter 18

Strife

In the last few chapters, I introduced the idea of demons falling into two categories, quiet or loud. What I mean by this is how a person reacts to being demonized can be heard as the demonic spirit begins to work through the person. Strife, like Bitterness, is a loud spirit. We don't use the word strife a lot in today's vocabulary, so let's go over exactly what we mean by "strife".

Strife is a strong and ongoing conflict over a fundamental issue. Strife is deeper than argument, broader than disagreement. Strife usually involves bitterness and sometimes violence. Someone who is demonized by a Spirit of Strife will direct it at others, and where you see this most hurtful is in marriages. My initial inspiration on this topic was because of what we see play out in marriages or familial relationships. As we move to understand how this demon works against us, I want you to be open to understanding our reactions and how our actions create reactions in others while remembering we are wanting to clear out things and evict the enemy influence in our lives.

The Demon of Strife will typically be the strongman, and with it we will generally see the demons of contention, bickering, argument, quarreling and fighting. There may also be some sides of witchcraft and control coming out as someone uses manipulation to get their way in an argument. The main challenge with this particular strongman is that no matter what the end result is, they are not satisfied. You could end up compromising with someone who has a demon of strife, and it will never be good enough because they would still rather have the argument than get their way and have peace. You cannot win in this because there is no end to allow for a win. The subject matter will just rotate onto something else. Think of a Ferris wheel. You never get off of it, you just keep switching seats.

Let's take a look at what the Bible tells us about strife.

Proverbs 13:10, "*Where there is strife, there is pride, but wisdom is found in those who take advice.*"

Proverbs 17:1, "*Better a dry crust with peace and quiet than a house full of feasting, with strife.*"

Proverbs 18:6, "*The lips of fools bring them strife, and their mouths invite a beating.*"

Proverbs 20:3, "*It is to one's honor to avoid strife, but every fool is quick to quarrel.*"

Proverbs 22:10, "*Drive out the mocker, and out goes strife; quarrels and insults are ended.*"

Proverbs 26:21, "*As charcoal to embers and as wood to fire, so is a quarrelsome person for kindling strife.*"

A look at scripture gives us a pretty good idea that strife will lead us absolutely nowhere.

I know someone who from all appearance's sake has an issue with strife. I would not say I am friends with him, but I know him. We'll go ahead and just call him, John. For about the last two years I have been noticing that John likes to say things that are intended to skewer people. He couches it under the pretense of using scripture as a way to speak truth to people, but that is not actually what he is doing. He references a scripture and then proceeds to pontificate for quite a while on his thoughts on the scripture and why everybody out there is going to hell. He literally said this. I want to add that the audience he is speaking to are Christians, and he is talking about Christians. I generally try to ignore him, not because I don't want the conflict but because usually these types of people just want attention and to be held in high regard and by ignoring him, I am simply dismissing his discussions. Conflict for me is not an issue, I don't shy away from that when it is the right thing to do. About a year or two ago, it was sometime in October, it was on a Sunday, I just couldn't ignore him. He was attacking Christians who had second marriages in a blanket statement and that particular day I had just had enough of his rhetoric. Not everyone who was hearing his words was a mature Christian, and it was confusing new believers who were in second marriages. Many times, when he speaks, he is not biblically sound and not only was he not biblically sound on this topic, but the way he was choosing to address people about it was just too far out of bounds for me to not address it. He was saying things in a way to shame them. So, I started my response to him in such a way to give him a chance to back out of the condemning position he had taken and asked him what was his purpose in what he was saying. I asked if he was trying to hit Christians with a stick or was he just being self-righteous. I told him it was not his job to pass judgment on these people and that if someone is remarried, they answer to Jesus, and they can continue to have a fruitful life. I also indicated that there will likely be people in heaven who have remarried with a crown more adorned than his. I told him to stop creating this confusion among his own brothers and sisters in Christ and cautioned him to ask the Lord about what he should be saying before he says it. I explained that if he did that, he would likely find that he had less to say. Unbelievably, or believably, he doubled down and told me that no one who is in a second marriage will go to heaven, and that I must believe in a liberal God who lets sin slide and that was my choice.

Now that type of response is indicative of someone who just wants to continue to argue. Someone who has to always be right. So, I responded with "that type of response further illustrated his immaturity in Christ and that what he said was not Holy Spirit inspired and certainly was not how Jesus would respond. I told him I thought he needed to study the Bible more and look at how Jesus ministered to people. I encouraged him to understand his role, and how the Holy Spirit would carry it out, and that his responses were not Christ centered. John didn't like that either, and he called me a Pharisee, which makes zero sense - zero. What I was saying was about as anti-Pharisaical as it gets. He said if Jesus were here, I would say Jesus was not being Christ centered and that he was being mean. Again, it made no sense. He then told me the truth will convict me and not accepting the truth doesn't change the truth. My next response was simple. He was missing the point and if he continues to do things his way instead of the Holy Spirit's way, one day he will see he is not yielding fruit as Christ did. At that point someone else spoke up and continued to correct him on his biblical stance.

When I think of John, I wonder what motivates him to be so, well what comes across as, hateful to other Christians. Can you imagine John coming at a non-believer? It's no wonder so many people hate Christians when that's what they get to experience. I understand what John thought he was doing; he just went about it all wrong and, in my opinion, had the enemy influencing him as he did it. I think if John would have been doing that in front of Paul in the first century, Paul's response would have been swift to correct him as well.

Let's take a look at what Paul wrote about people like John who want constant friction, or strife.

1 Timothy 6:2-5, *"These are the things you are to teach and insist on.* *³ If anyone teaches otherwise and does not agree to the sound instruction of our Lord Jesus Christ and to godly teaching, they are conceited and understand nothing. They have an unhealthy interest in controversies and quarrels about words that result in envy,* **strife**, *malicious talk, evil suspicions and constant friction between people of corrupt mind, who have been robbed of the truth and who think that godliness is a means to financial gain."*

John may not have been seeking financial gain in all the strife he has caused in the past, but his interest in creating controversy certainly applies. John has admitted he is trying to start his own church because he doesn't agree with anything the pastors say at the churches he has attended. No matter where John goes or what he creates, it will result in a lack of fruit and in chaos because of the demonic influence he not only allows but continues to encourage and feed.

We can't let strife enter our lives and dictate how we then interact with people. When it is occurring in marriages, it is truly sad. Sometimes we put our spouses' feelings below the feelings of others because we know they will still be there even if we treat them poorly, or we do that to our parents or our children because maybe they can't leave. That's a horrible attitude to take. We need to wake up and see our spouse, our children or our parents as Christ sees them. The enemy will do whatever it takes to destroy relationships and tear apart families. Strife is a well-known way to do that.

Paul says this in Romans 1:29, "*They have become filled with every kind of wickedness, evil, greed and depravity. They are full of envy, murder, **strife**, deceit and malice. They are gossips, slanderers, God-haters, insolent, arrogant and boastful; they invent ways of doing evil; they disobey their parents;* [31] *they have no understanding, no fidelity, no love, no mercy.* [32] *Although they know God's righteous decree that those who do such things deserve death, they not only continue to do these very things but also approve of those who practice them.*"

If we think we have some strife in our lives, how do we evict it? Well, we first need to acknowledge it. In acknowledging it, I would also examine in what relationships are you exhibiting strife? Is it only your marriage? Is it only at work? Is it everywhere, in all your relationships? You want to know this because you want to get to the root of why you are creating this in your relationships. Has your spouse done things, and this is your default reaction? We can't pay back wrong with wrong; it won't work. Were you passed over for a promotion at work? Have you asked the Lord if that is the promotion He wanted for you? Are your kids acting out so all you can do is yell? Figure out what you can control with one area and work on that as a start.

Let's go through the 5 steps to evict strife:

1. Acknowledge it: We can't hide it or hide from it.

2. Understand it: What is driving it? What relationship? Is it our reaction? Be honest with yourself in this step or you will find yourself dealing with this over and over again.
3. Address it: Either work through it with the person or work through the situation driving it
4. Release it to the Lord and don't try to take it back from Him later
5. Replace the void with the peace of the Holy Spirit. If we are going to evict the enemy and his influence, we need to replace it and fill ourselves with what the Holy Spirit provides. Use your scriptures as you pray to help you gain strength.

I want to also give you some scriptures to start with for support in the eviction process.

If we look at the Armor of God, in Ephesians 6:15, "*and having shod your feet with the gospel of peace.*" We see that peace is part of what we need for spiritual warfare, which is a part of the eviction process.

We are given the fruits of the spirit in Galatians 5:22, "*But the fruit of the Spirit is love, joy, peace, longsuffering, kindness, goodness, faithfulness*"

Paul tells us in Romans 16:20, "*And the God of peace shall bruise Satan under your feet shortly. The grace of our Lord Jesus Christ be with you.*"

Again, in Romans 15:33, "*Now the God of peace be with you all*"

And in Romans 8:6, *For the mind of the flesh is death; but the mind of the Spirit is life and peace"*

And finally in Romans 5:1, *"Being therefore justified by faith, we have **peace** with God through our Lord Jesus Christ;"*

Chapter 19

Worry

The Spirit of Worry is both a strongman and a quiet spirit. It wants to work in the background to eat away at us slowly before we realize it has a foothold. Not every circumstance of worry is a demonic attack or is indicative of a demonic influence. Again, we don't have a demon around every corner but there are some instances where the demon of worry is hard at work, and we can fall prey to the manipulation. Let's dig deeper into the demon of worry, who it hangs out with it, and how to know when we are just being worrisome (which we still need to change) versus being demonization.

The Spirit of Worry will take those deep things in our hearts and use them to mentally, emotionally, and physically cripple us to do or not do what is necessary to move through our worry. Often with the Spirit of Worry you will find the Spirit of Fear, the Spirit of Anxiety, Dread and the Spirit of Apprehension. They all work well together to paralyze us and keep us from hearing from the Lord. I want to share with you some indications that you might be experiencing demonization or the beginnings of demonization which is the influence of the spirit of worry and its associates.

Worry will influence you to be:

1. Unable to sleep: This attack at night is intended to inhibit our rest to keep us imbalanced. If they can deprive us of enough sleep, then we are not able to think clearly, and it will affect other areas of our lives significantly. Often the use of nightmares will keep us from wanting to sleep.

2. Unable to eat: This attack is meant to position us to begin to have cognitive and physical issues and begin breaking us down physically. We become more vulnerable and unable to fight or even defend ourselves.

3. Unable to make decisions or process thoughts logically: Attacking our decision making and thought process will keep us from remaining in reality and ultimately, we will not maintain our responsibilities which will affect others around us. Confusion and Paranoia could begin to creep in over time.

4. Unable to control emotions: Worry and its associates can position us to feel that everything is coming against us, and we cannot stand. When we have no composure, we are weak and cannot defend ourselves or discern correctly what is coming against us.

5. Isolation from others: Pulling back and no longer having social support is a huge red flag! You become more vulnerable when you are on your own, and you will begin to believe the lies the enemy tells you because you will begin to lose perspective.

Many times, when we are struggling with worry, it is over a specific situation: loss of a job, a struggling marriage, health of a family member, or even trying to find a place to live. Those are all relatable. We all understand how stressful those situations can become. We ask for prayer; we talk to our friends or our pastor. Those are life events. That's not really what we are talking about here. You could have lost your job and as a result you are so worried about feeding your family you can't sleep nor can you eat. That is understandable. We should still turn to the Lord in all circumstances, but we would expect those life situations to be temporary not prolonged. I know marriages may be in turmoil for years and therefore prolonged, but there is generally something behind that situation other than the spirit of worry. What we are talking about here are situations where the spirit of worry is allowed freedom beyond the temporary situations to the prolonged.

In 2022, I had a situation in my own life that if I did not have the relationship with the Lord that I have, I would have easily been in a situation where I was filled with worry, anxiety and uncertainty.

As I've shared before about my eldest son and his stroke, here is a little more about his story. In the beginning of March 2022, my son went to an in-person work event and unfortunately like so many people, got COVID. While he has always been healthy with no comorbidities or anything to indicate there might be any issues, he did get a really intense cough that lingered for weeks. Once he finally got to where he felt better on April 2nd, he went to get a haircut and physical therapy for his neck because he was feeling intense pain in the back of his neck. In the hours following that therapy appointment - he had a major stroke. The month of April contained three brain surgeries and three long weeks in ICU, which provided us with some intense moments especially surrounding the one specific where everyone thought he was not going to survive. It was a very difficult

187

time, I never missed a day by his side to help him as he navigated being intubated, being restrained against his will, learning to walk again, regaining his memory of what year it was, where he lived and even who he was. There were some really sweet moments of realization as we shared pictures with him of his life, his dogs, and the music he likes. In many ways, he grew up again before my eyes because in the beginning stages he was very childlike. From ICU he went straight to rehab to learn how to dress, to shower and all the things he needed to be able to take care of himself safely. He progressed well and transitioned to the use of a walker and then was released to continue to recover at home. We knew that the stint that was placed in his brain on one side was working, but we also knew the right side of his brain was receiving no blood. There are still a few side effects periodically and a handful of things he won't be able to do again, like ride a roller coaster, which is fine.

About 6 months after he was released from the hospital, my son had an appointment for a surgical procedure to allow the surgeon to look and see how his brain has accepted the stint, how the right side was doing, how the two front arteries were fairing. I learned from the first day he arrived at the ER, which was April 3rd, that I needed to trust what the Lord said about the outcome but also to be prepared for whatever happens until you get to the outcome. The events of a circumstance do not dictate the outcome. As soon as I found out he was in the ER, I asked the Lord about it. He told me that he would survive, and he would come out of it even better. I never really clued in on the use of the words "he will survive." I actually just took it as the Lord saying he would be okay. It wasn't until six hours later that I realized something was really wrong, and this was a life-threatening situation for him. At that moment, I knew I had the Lord telling me, he would survive, and as we went through all of the events I described, and some of them were very, very intense difficult moments, I just knew no matter what - he was going to survive and be better than he was.

So fast forward to the night before his follow up procedure. I was spending time with the Lord. The Lord pointed out that my heart was heavy. He told me to let go of it; the heaviness was not mine to bear. He also told me that my son was His, and He adored him. A few minutes later my son called with an updated time to be at the hospital, and we prayed. I felt so much better afterwards. The Lord comforted me, even though I didn't bring it up to Him, and I heard from my son pretty immediately and was able to pray over him which was relaxing. I know my son was somewhat uncomfortable and apprehensive with the procedure and not knowing what to expect and the prayer helped him.

I am sharing with you what the Lord gave me. For me, remembering a situation where I am having to reflect on a very intense and faith challenging period of my life is not comfortable. During that time, I knew worry, anxiety, fear, dread and apprehension were not far off, but I also knew I could not allow it to preoccupy my time and still be able to stand on what the Lord gave me months ago as the final word over this entire situation. I am not telling you anything which I have not walked out myself. I am speaking from experience. Life has moments when we are scared and don't know or don't understand what is happening. I want to help you be prepared for anything. I want you to rely on the Lord and seek Him in all circumstances, the good and the bad. Because when the unexpected comes, you will then naturally lean into Him and get guidance and understanding. Trusting in Him is the beginning of life.

To tackle worry, I have put together six steps to help you rid yourselves of the influence of the Spirit of Worry. You can use these same steps for the Spirits as well, Anxiety, Fear, Dread, and Apprehension. Applying these six steps to the temporary situations will provide support from the Lord but also prevent it all from becoming prolonged worry situations. When we allow the enemy a place in our lives, we give it the legal right to influence your life in those places.

6 Steps to Rid ourselves of the influence from the Spirit of Worry:
1. Acknowledge it: Admitting that you have the issue with worry is important so you can begin the eviction process. Hiding it or not being willing to admit it allows it the right to remain, and it will continue to build.
2. Rebuke! Rebuke! Rebuke!: Tell the enemy it has to leave in Jesus' name. You must be willing to evict all of it. Take control of the situation; you have the authority. They don't.
3. Repent: Turn to the Lord for your support to live by what the Word says, not what the enemy says. Use scriptures.
   a. Psalm 56:3, "When I am afraid, I put my trust in you."
   b. Proverbs 10:24, *"what the wicked dread will overtake them; what the righteous desire will be granted."*
   c. Isaiah12:2, Surely God is my salvation; I will trust and not be afraid. The Lord, the

Lord himself is my strength and my
defense; he has become my salvation."

4. Understand: Take some time and begin to identify
   what and why you allowed yourself to be ruled by
   worry. How long has it been going on? How did you
   feed it? Ask the Lord to reveal to you the ways He
   can guide you. This is important so you can discern
   when it is creeping up again, and you can rebuke it
   again and again.

5. Release it to the Lord: Give it all to Him and do not
   allow yourself to hold on to any worry.

   a. 1 Peter 5:7, *"Cast all your anxiety on him
      because he cares for you."*

   b. Matthew 6:27, *"Can any one of you by worrying
      add a single hour to your life?"*

   c. Matthew 6:25-26, "Therefore I tell you, do
      not worry about your life, what you will eat
      or drink; or about your body, what you will
      wear. Is not life more than food, and the
      body more than clothes? Look at the birds
      of the air; they do not sow or reap or store
      away in barns, and yet your heavenly
      Father feeds them. Are you not much more
      valuable than they?

   d. Matthew 6:33, "Therefore do not worry
      about tomorrow, for tomorrow will worry
      about itself. Each day has enough trouble
      of its own.

6. Replace it: Worry is a failure to Trust God, so we
   need to replace worry with Trust.

a. Isaiah 26:4 "Trust in the Lord forever, for the Lord, the Lord himself is the Rock eternal."
b. Proverbs 3:5, "Trust in the Lord with all your heart and lean not on your own understanding."
c. Psalm 56:4, "In God, whose word I praise- in God I trust and am not afraid. What can mere mortals do to me."
d. Isaiah 26:3, "You will keep in perfect peace those whose minds are steadfast, because they trust in you."
e. Romans 15:13, "May the God of hope fill you with all joy and peace as you trust in him, so that you may overflow with hope by the power of the Holy Spirit.

Chapter 20

Impatience

The Spirit of Impatience, I would consider a loud spirit. It starts out as a quiet spirit, but as it builds, it can't help but let itself be known whether it be in word or in action. Impatience is, by definition, a lack of patience. I will say, not all impatience is a demonic influence. There is a difference between someone who has a lack of patience and someone who is demonized by the Spirit of Impatience. The Spirit of Impatience can demonize someone who is patient, so we need to understand the difference so we can identify and recognize when the Spirit of Impatience has made an appearance and is attempting to influence us and tempt us into actions that manifest demonization.

The Spirit of Impatience will generally be the Strongman and will often be accompanied by the Spirit of Agitation, The Spirit of Frustration, the Spirit of Intolerance, the Spirit of Resentment, the Spirit of Criticism. Impatience begins to have an influence over us, develops over time quietly and then pulls in one of the other demons to manifest even uglier behavior. That's where colorful behavior and the "loudness" become apparent. When we become agitated, we start to see our actions speak by slamming things, throwing things, breaking things, or speaking rudely. It's like a little volcano starting to percolate, and if we can't get past it, the explosion occurs. We talked about resentment and the role it can play when we discussed bitterness. These seven demons in this series are entangled together so we will see them in multiple environments.

Tangled with the Spirit of Impatience is the Spirit of Criticism. It will frequently show up in marriages and other familial relationships. It is extremely common because people we spend the most time with will likely be the ones who we become most impatient with if we are experiencing something with them over and over. As the Spirit of Impatience works to grate on us, percolating, the Spirit of Criticism is readying itself for that explosion, but it won't be a huge one-time Mt Vesuvius event. It will be over time with smaller eruptions of tearing someone else apart through our words. The end result is the same as if it were Mt Vesuvius; you are slowly killing the sweet spirit of people around you with your harsh words.

The Spirit of Intolerance has gained immense power in the last five years. It snuck up on us, and now there is a strong Spirit of Impatience across the globe that produces a level of Intolerance which is deadly. The enemy has raised up people all over the world with a Spirit of Impatience for what they want, and for their wanting it now. If we don't all agree with whatever it is they want, then the Spirit of Intolerance comes out and uses hate, twists everything to make it appear anyone and everyone else is intolerant.

The Spirit of Frustration builds off Impatience, starting out quietly and then building to an eventual explosion as well. Unlike the Spirit of Criticism which tends to be more focused on specific targets, Frustration is directed everywhere. More of a blitzkrieg, if you will. I will readily admit that I am an impatient person. I do not have a Spirit of Impatience demonizing me, but I can for sure see where I have had that in the past. A lot of times you will see the demonization occurring more in type A personalities. It is easy for this Spirit to attack these people because there are easy opportunities, readily available like hanging fruit. I used to be a Type A personality when I was younger. I still have the tendencies, but being more experienced in life and having more wisdom, I know when to step back and work with things out of my control rather than try to fight against things out of my control that I don't like. I will never be a Type B personality. My sister was more type B, it always struck me at how opposite we were having the same parents, same DNA essentially in terms of our genetics. We could not have been more opposite in personality, appearance, interests. She rode a motorcycle, had her leather ensembles. I enjoy the safety of the metal surrounding me in my car. I will say, my dad also forbade us to even sit on a motorcycle as a kid; they were too dangerous. So, imagine my surprise when my sister got a motorcycle, and then unbeknownst to me, my dad gets one as well and, I think they even rode together. I am digressing, but the point I am finally making here is people change. So, if you find yourself dealing with impatience and you are not dealing with it as gracefully as you would like, you can change it. Whether it is due to demonization or not, we can all change.

Let's see what the Bible tells us about Impatience and how will you know if you are just impatient versus being influenced by the Spirit of Impatience. When we want to understand how the Lord sees impatience, we need to look at what the Bible says regarding patience, the virtues associated with it, and in which direction His truth guides us.

195

We will start off with the anchors that Paul gives us for Godly character, Galatians 5:22, *"But the fruit of the Spirit is love, joy, peace, forbearance, kindness, goodness, faithfulness, gentleness and self-control."* If we had any doubt of the importance of patience, this verse should settle that. A Godly character includes patience.

Here is Paul again encouraging us in how to treat each other. Ephesians 4:2, *"Be completely humble and gentle; be patient, bearing with one another in love."*

Psalm 37:7, *"Be still before the LORD and wait patiently for him; do not fret when people succeed in their ways, when they carry out their wicked schemes."* How many people are praying and seeking an answer from the Lord, but won't wait patiently for Him to answer, and instead move ahead in their own plan. It won't work that way.

Proverbs 14:29, *" Whoever is patient has great understanding, but one who is quick-tempered displays folly."* The Lord will give us great understanding, but this indicates someone with a quick temper will not receive that and instead behaves foolishly.

Proverbs 15:18, *"A hot-tempered person stirs up conflict, but the one who is patient calms a quarrel."* Same concept as the previous proverb. The temper invites strife.

Proverbs 16:32, *"Better a patient person than a warrior, one with self-control than one who takes a city."*

This next one is one of my favorites; I quote it frequently. When I am waiting on the Lord, this is a good one as a reminder for myself. Also, this is a great defensive and offensive weapon. If you feel the enemy is provoking you or even your own will is working against you, take authority over it all and use this scripture. Just because we don't think we have an answer - and I say that meaning the Lord may have responded but we missed it because we wanted what we wanted and were not open to what His best provides, but this will help to put things into perspective and cool your jets so to speak. Romans 8:25, *"But if we hope for what we do not yet have, we wait for it patiently."*

Romans 12:12, *" Be joyful in hope, patient in affliction, faithful in prayer."* Patient in affliction is master level self-control. We should strive to be at this level. When everything is out of your control and you need a movement from the Lord, but are waiting on Him, master level patience is at work.

1 Corinthians 13:4, *" Love is patient, love is kind. It does not envy, it does not boast, it is not proud."* This is important for those dealing with a spirit of criticism. Generally, if you are criticizing, it is because you think your way is better than someone else's. Whether it is or not, pull back the criticism and allow the other person to have some free will, dignity and time to improve if they need to with good guidance.

Hebrews 6:15, *"And so after waiting patiently, Abraham received what was promised."* I love this scripture because it is evidence that if we wait on the Lord, He will come through. He has for centuries from Abraham's day to now.

2 Peter 3:9, *"The Lord is not slow in keeping his promise, as some understand slowness. Instead he is patient with you, not wanting anyone to perish, but everyone to come to repentance."* This one is always a good one to review because it essentially is reminding us that the Lord is patient with us as we make our mistakes and behave in ways dishonoring to Him and others. He doesn't

yell at us, He corrects us, but He does it in a loving way and we need to exhibit the same behavior in how we relate to others. I know we don't want the Lord to treat us the way we treat others at times.

Patience is mentioned so many times to us, and these scriptures are only a snapshot, but it is mentioned to us because for many patience is a struggle. The enemy has many opportunities to use it against us if we let him. So how can you tell the difference between patience just as an area we need to build up in our character or as demonization? We are going to use the scripture as our guide. In all cases, based on Galatians 5:22, we know that Patience is a trait we need to develop in our character.

When our impatience is bringing in other sin areas, we can start to get an idea there is a demon influencing us. Here are ten questions you can ask yourself about your behavior and your level of impatience to determine if you are being affected by a demonic influence:

1. Is your impatience leading you to argue and create conflicts with others?
2. Is your impatience beginning to create seeds of resentment toward others?
3. Does your impatience cause you to say things that tear others apart?
4. Is your impatience creating a chasm in your relationship with the Lord?
5. Do you behave in ways you are ashamed of or embarrassed by later?
6. Are you having to apologize for your behavior after the fact?

7. Does it cause you to behave in ways you wouldn't otherwise but for the impatience?
8. Are you creating divides in your marriage, family or any other relationships because of how you behave as a result of being impatient?
9. Do others avoid you or steer clear of certain conversations in your presence?
10. Do you ever feel like you are not able to control yourself when you get impatient?

If the answer to two or more of these questions is yes, then you may be experiencing some level of demonization. It will continue to grow if you are not willing to address it and make changes.

If you answer no, but still want to improve how you handle impatience, here are five steps to begin change:

1. Acknowledge it: we can't pretend, others around us already know
2. Understand it: what is driving it, what relationships or areas trigger you?
3. Address it: Think ahead, how will you stop yourself when you feel triggered? What action can you take as it occurs?
4. Release it to the Lord: Take whatever occurred, whatever is triggering you and hand it over to Him and let go of it. Sometimes we hand it over and forget to let go of it.
5. Replace it: Impatience can be difficult to shift gears immediately, so you must first stop and be still. Invite the Holy Spirit to help you

maintain control. You are working to shift from impatience to kindness and love. That's a huge shift for some so it will take time. If we are going to evict the enemy and his influence, we need to replace impatience and fill ourselves with what the Holy Spirit provides. Use your scriptures as you pray to help you gain strength. If you are struggling with replacing it, go back and check if you completed step 4.

Chapter 21

Religion

The Spirit of Religion has a pronounced impact on our relationship with the Holy Spirit. Often accompanying the Spirit of Religion is the Spirit of Accusation and the Spirit of Perfection. This lethal combination has damaged the church for centuries and continues to grow causing Christians, who are allowing themselves to be limited by these spirits, to cannibalize the move of the Holy Spirit in the church today.

Religious Spirits are really a family of spirits where the strongman is the Religious Spirit. The family generally includes legalism, religiosity, traditionalism, formalism, doctrinal obsession, doctrinal error, fear of God, fear of losing salvation, lawfulness, obsession with being right, lack of tolerance for correction, and is works based. This is not an exhaustive list, but it gives you a pretty clear picture of where these demons are leading people. In these types of beliefs, a Christian does not allow for the Holy Spirit to work and move, but instead creates a place where the individual has to work, and sometimes that means to work for their salvation.

These spirits are typically the ones that serve to drive people away from attending church. This is not a loving atmosphere, but rather a strict guideline, and adherence to that guideline is what is considered important. This thinking does not allow for people to come as they are because it already has in mind how they should be when they get there. All the activities are built on their belief system which may have some seed of biblical application, but by and large, are manmade guidelines or requirements in some denominations. There is sometimes punishment if one steps outside of the manmade requirements. This is different from the biblical church discipline that Paul describes in 1 Corinthians.

The Spirit of Religion creates in us a legalist mentality. Let us look closer at a how a legalist functions. A legalist does not seek to rightly obey and apply every word of the Bible to their own life, but insists others comply. A legalist is someone who disobeys the Bible by adding to the Bible human rules and regulations for thought, life, and morality, and then proceeds to judge themselves and others by these self-made rules.

I see these religious spirits play out a lot outside of the church as well. When someone with marital discord seeks counsel from a fellow Christian, I have seen some extremely harsh words come out condemning the person for even reaching out, then further slamming them by questioning why they are having issues. Where I see this most often and it is incredibly harmful, is when advice is being given to those in a second marriage. In the last few weeks - maybe 2 or 3, I have seen at least five people reach out wanting support from a Christian marriage support group. I am a member of this group and have become extremely disappointed at some of the advice being given. All five of these cases involved a second marriage and all were long-term marriages - in the twenty year range for the second marriage. The issues ran the gamut on severity. There is another member who gives advice and says the same thing to every single one of these people. He essentially says this, "Could the reason you are having these marital issues be the fact that the spouse (whichever or both if it's a second marriage for both) is still biblically married to their previous spouse, and you or the other spouse, whichever, is actually committing adultery by being with them? From there he has a huge list of scriptures he uses to tell them they are living in sin, and the marriage is not blessed by God. He does not take the time to find out why they are in a second marriage. In his eyes, every second marriage is a blanket sin, and therefore God will not honor it by helping them resolve their issues and stay married. So, it doesn't matter why they are in a second marriage; it's a sin. That type of thinking and attitude is purely demonic - a religious spirit, and they are using what they think is a biblical doctrine to really kick these people when they are down already. Where did Jesus ever do that? Using the Bible (incorrectly mind you) as an excuse to beat people up is essentially what the Pharisees and the Sadducees were doing, and that is what Jesus fought against. An organization filled with people who have no heart, no willingness to listen and understand and only serve to use the Bible to hurt and not heal or guide is an organization that is dead.

As far as that marriage advice group is concerned, I did speak up about how these people were being treated by this individual, and that this individual in particular was misusing scripture. He wasn't the only one, but he was always the first to speak up. I had a long discussion but unfortunately, I was told he was using scripture in his response so he could voice his opinion. My response was that if you let this continue then you are condoning a misuse and even in some cases an abuse of scripture. I stepped back from participating and to my surprise, the same person who told me the opinion of the scripture abuser was okay, began to say the exact same things I was saying about his responses. She even stated he omitted pertinent words from his scriptural references. It shouldn't be this hard to speak the truth.

Another aspect I have seen of the religious spirit is in four women I have recently been meeting with, and I have seen in all four cases - the use of shame and guilt. From each woman I heard the same words of how the religious spirit working actively in family and church members made them feel they are not able to be loved. Understand how these spirits work on us. They will make you think, and erroneously believe, you are incapable of being loved because you can never measure up to what you are being told you need to do. This in turn produces self-hatred and self-condemnation no matter what your accomplishments or how hard you "work." This demonic influence uses a rule-based mentality and creates a series of rules that are impossible to keep because in many cases they are contradictory. When you are rules based, you cannot function in love. These demons will influence you to hate the fruit of love. Without love, they can keep you in spiritual bondage with self-condemnation knowing if you cannot love yourself, you cannot love others. If you cannot love others, then you can't develop relationships and this does not just extend to those around you, but also in your relationship with Jesus, with God, with the Holy Spirit. This demonic influence stresses performance over relationship, and when it can get you to a place where you think you failed, then you cannot develop relationships that will lead you to freedom in Christ.

When we add to God's word that is legalism. So, what is the opposite of legalism that is also not in alignment with God? Rebellion. What I see happening in the lives of the people I talk with who have been dealing with the fallout of legalist churches or family members is a spirit of rebellion developing. It looks similar to the fight or flight response we face when we encounter danger. Rebellion is the fight aspect.

One of the women I am working with now has a very heightened level of fight so that even when she wants to submit to Jesus, she is fighting it because she is having issues trusting that God is going to walk beside her, even when she knows he already is walking beside her. He has made some unbelievable changes in her life a reality and she still struggles to let her rebellion go fully of her rebellion. We had lunch a few weeks ago and she looked at me and said, "I want to get closer to God; I want to hear His voice, I want to know what He wants for me in my life. I know I have to get all of this demonic influence out of my life, but I am fighting myself." She was still in her rebellion mode from what happened to her as she grew up and from the religious spirits in her family that forced her to make decisions based on what family members wanted her to do - not what she was ready to do. As she talked, you could see her blood pressure increase. She became more animated; her volume increased; her neck turned red; her relaxed smile became an angry smile as she spoke. She was so tired of carrying around all of this weight and wanted to be free of it once and for all. She just couldn't get rid of it no matter what she tried. So, let's talk about why it is hard to rid ourselves of this kind of baggage and evict the enemy.

To do that, let's move on to the Spirit of Accusation. Have you ever had someone accuse you of something you didn't do, and just wouldn't let it go? They kept hounding you and telling other people, damaging your name and reputation. If that is happening to you, you are likely doing all you can to clear your name, to prove you didn't do whatever or even to confront the person telling lies. It's a terrible position to be in because you know that it's likely you will never be able to put yourself back in the position you were in before the false accusations started.

Now imagine if you did do something, but not what you are being accused of, but you don't know how to defend yourself. You are less likely to be able to speak up. What if you did it, but you made the situation right, and you are living correctly already. People in these situations find it harder to clear their name, and this is exactly how the enemy wants you to feel. Even after you accepted Jesus' forgiveness, the enemy drags it back up again. The enemy will take everything you do and twist it and make it sound unforgivable, will pick you apart, and if he sees it is working, then it goes at you harder. That is Accusation.

Accusation…This spirit functions by using Judgment, Criticism, and Faultfinding in everything you do. It will twist your motives and make you question your beliefs in the Bible. A small mistake will look like an insurmountable mountain. You can't move past it; you keep dwelling on it week after week second guessing what you should have done instead. It brings to mind that if you had been better, you would have reacted better. You would have made a better choice; you would not have handled that situation incorrectly. Then you must focus on how to correct it and all the while the enemy is telling you that nothing you do will actually correct it. So, you are really just being kept in a suspenseful state with all the what ifs and how tos. You aren't meant to find a way out of any of this. If you do manage to do so, well, that just starts a new cycle.

In Revelation 12:10, Jesus refers to Satan as our accuser, *"For the accuser of our brothers and sisters, who accuses them before our God day and night,".* The enemy enjoys listing our sins, continually bringing them up so we won't accept the forgiveness that Jesus provides. If we are continually having our sins placed before us, it makes it difficult to repent and trust in our relationship with Jesus. In that state, we can't see our Advocate, Jesus, as our defender and realize He is able to address the accusations against us. He paid the ultimate price for us. I John 2 tells us Jesus, the Righteous One, is the atoning sacrifice for our sins, covering us in all our transgressions. Accusation only wants to distract you and call you a failure in an attempt to put you on trial and punish you. This is why it pairs so well with the Spirit of Perfection.

The Spirit of Perfection is rampant in our world today. For many people, the only image they want to portray is the image that their life is perfect, they look perfec; they have the perfect house; the perfect job, car - whatever. The reality is, none of us have a perfect life. We cannot ever be perfect. We don't need to be. Jesus was, and we have Him so we don't need anything else. That's great if we have a nice house, but that doesn't mean you are any better than someone who doesn't have a nice house. When our time comes and we face the Lord, we can't say, "Lord, I may not have been very close to you, but I had the perfect house." The Bible does not tell us anywhere to be perfect; we are not striving for that. We want to be righteous, Christ like, but righteous and perfect are not the same thing, and righteous and self-righteous are not the same thing.

When dealing with the Spirit of Perfection, you are dealing with Pride, Vanity, Ego, Frustration, Criticism, Irritability, Intolerance, Anger, Impatience, need for approval, and the need for attention.

Remember the woman I spoke of previously who was dealing with rebellion? When we dug deeper into what was at the root of some of her issues, we also found the Spirit of Perfection. For years she was raised thinking she had to always be perfect. All of her activities, how she looked, how she behaved, her school choice, her degree choice, how she presented her family life had to be perfect. As she was talking to me about her frustrations and her expectations of God, I could see her rebellion taking her in the wrong direction. She was becoming critical of what she thought God did and of His judgment of people. It was really the religious spirit trying to push back against her trying to submit to God. For me, it was almost like watching a toddler trying to persuade a parent for some candy or something. If you have ever watched young children try different angles, it's a part of learning, a part of communication and negotiation, but when she was doing it, it wasn't cute. It was pointed, and it was against God. There were a few topics she was really stuck on, wondering how God could do such a thing or be such a way. As I listened, I could tell that her view of God was not actually who God is; it was who legalists say He is and demonstrated the hateful behaviors they exhibit. So, after we walked through that, I redirected the conversation to what we were actually talking about - her being raised thinking that she had to be the picture of Perfection. We talked about it for a few minutes and then I asked her point blank, "When did you achieve your perfection?" She looked at me and I could see her countenance change as she laughed and said, "Never." It was then she started to realize she, too, was placing expectations on herself she could not meet. She still felt like a failure no matter what she achieved. Her self-condemnation was on its way to eclipsing any expectations she felt her parents had of her - keep in mind - she is twenty-eight. Her need for approval has shifted over the years, but in the beginning, when she was young, it was very strong.

Allowing ourselves to be influenced to follow these demonic spirits will rob us of our experiences with the Holy Spirit. We will close ourselves off, sometimes feeling comfortable in the unpleasant conditions because at least we know what that is like. Fear of the unknown with the Holy Spirit means you won't know Him personally, you won't hear Him clearly, and you will stay just as you are, living less than the full life Jesus promises us in John 10:10.

Why are all three of these demonic influences extremely harmful?

Religious spirits, accusation, perfection - they all destroy from within and carry forward to damage the relationships you have with those around you. This works to isolate you and pull you away from God. It's a common and basic tactic the enemy uses to pull us down and pull us apart. We must see how they work against us to separate us so we can stop it as it comes to attack. We don't have to endure any of this if we maintain our focus on who God is and know who He isn't.

Chapter 22

Distraction

The Spirit of Distraction uses multiple strategies that are so subtle we don't even notice it until we are already distracted and sometimes, as a result, forget what we were originally doing. We often dismiss this as memory loss, or some people will claim they have ADHD or ADD to justify behavior. The Spirit of Distraction is real and very good at what it does. It sounds harmless enough, but its objective is not harmless by any means.

Who exactly is this demon? You don't hear a lot about the Spirit of Distraction, and that is actually part of how this demon works. It doesn't want you to know about him because that would defeat the purpose of his work. If he is doing his job correctly, you won't be able to follow through on understanding who he is because he can keep you focused elsewhere. If we are dealing with this demon, we will have issues with: focus, completing projects, following through on our commitments, remembering appointments and time management. This will inevitably create problems in our relationships, in our work responsibilities and prevent us from achieving personal goals. All of that is bad enough, but the real intention of this demon is to keep us from developing and maintaining our relationship with the Lord. Using those other areas of our life is the distraction that will keep our wheels spinning so we don't read the Bible, pray, go to church, or go to Bible study. These are essentially, all the things we need in our lives to keep ourselves in order and our relationship close with the Lord which enables us to hear His voice above the Spirit of Distraction.

This demon will frequently be seen working together with the demons of frustration, forgetfulness, confusion, indifference, procrastination, and restlessness.

Let's look at some Biblical examples where we can see this demon at work.

In Genesis 3, we see the distraction of Eve unfold. To give some context to the situation, Eve was made to be a helper for Adam, and Adam's responsibility was the Garden of Eden. Adam was to work the Garden of Eden and take care of it. Eve should have been busy at work tending to Garden activities. The Bible doesn't tell us what their responsibilities were, but we do know it was a sizeable area because it supported all the animals. Eve's role was to be a helper in the Garden of Eden so she had areas she was meant to be focusing on in the Garden. At the time she was tempted by Satan she was alone, so that leads me to believe that Adam was somewhere working. They would likely have spent their downtime together. While alone, she would be more vulnerable than when Adam was there. We are all usually stronger when we have someone else there; the Bible even tells us that. So likely, she was on her own working, and she was distracted by Satan. The first distraction was very costly to her personally. It changed her life immediately with her resulting spiritual death and her life in terms of pain in childbearing. Even the land given to them was then cursed. Once they were ousted from the Garden of Eden, I can only imagine the amount of regret she had.

Now let's take a look at Samson. To read about Samson, we need to go into Judges, and his story starts at Chapter 13. The Israelites have been misbehaving, and God delivered them into the hands of the Philistines for forty years. Samson was God's answer to ending that judgment. God took a barren woman and blessed her with a son who was to be treated differently from the moment he was conceived. Throughout his life, Samson had the spirit of the Lord with him. Unfortunately, he still made some mistakes and misjudgments and allowed himself to be distracted. His relationship with the Lord was severed as a result of poor judgment in his relationship with Delilah, which we read about in Judges 16:20. He made the mistake of telling Delilah how God gave him his strength even after she had betrayed him three times. When the Lord left Samson, his strength left him as well and some pretty torturous things happened to Samson as a result. In the end, he did kill thousands of Philistines, but he died along with them. Allowing the distraction of Delilah and then all the continual distractions she caused, led him to a terrible end.

Let's now take a look at David. We are going to go to 2 Samuel 11 for this story. Let's set the scene: It is spring, the men of Israel are at war and David, their King, isn't where he is supposed to be - which is at war with them. Instead he is at home. He gets distracted when he sees Bathsheba. He wants her, but she is married to one of his men. David doesn't care; he sends for her, does what he wants to do, and ultimately Bathsheba gets pregnant. As a result, David does multiple things to try to cover up his sin and ends up adding more sin to the mix and ultimately creates a huge mess for himself by plotting to get Bathsheba's husband killed to help cover up the pregnancy. God isn't happy. He sends Nathan to rebuke David and tell him the consequences. The baby dies, the

213

household is sent into chaos, which consequently also affects the entire kingdom of Israel.

David allowed himself to be distracted. His relationship with the Lord was disrupted and the consequences were permanent. Innocent lives were lost. David was not the only one to pay the price for the sins that followed his distraction.

We know these Bible stories, but what does that mean for us today? We have WAY more opportunities to be distracted today. Our cell phones alone offer endless hours of escape, hours of entertainment, ways to do things we shouldn't, ways to shop, ways to learn. Not all the opportunities are negative, but they also can be a distraction if we are not careful.

This past weekend I was in a prayer meeting. At my church before the service, a group meets for prayer, and we do soaking where we have a specific focus and ask the Lord about it. It is not a typical prayer time. No one is speaking because we are focused and waiting on the Lord, or writing out what the Lord said to us individually and we share at the end. The room we are in is used for the middle schoolers after we leave. This past week during the payer time, no less than five different people came in the room to open or adjust a window. Everybody went to the same window, seemingly to do the same thing. Two other people came in the room looking around for something else. Two people came in late. One person brought in a kid about five years old who isn't at an age where he could sit still and be quiet to allow the rest of the room to have our prayer time. The room was full of distractions. I've never seen so many people in and out of a room that is supposed to be quiet and focused. This isn't me complaining; it's me describing a scenario for you to understand what was happening this past Sunday that doesn't normally happen. I will say, from the moment I walked in the room, I knew something was going to be off that morning. There was an interfering presence, but I didn't know why or where it was coming from, so I decided to keep that to myself and just wait to see what happened. Wherever God wants to move, the enemy does as well to keep us from moving with God and fulfilling His plans.

No one, anywhere is immune to distractions. How we respond to them is what we need to address.

Earlier this year I was doing a deliverance with a woman, we'll call her Jane, and it was probably one of the more severe cases I have seen. As we were beginning the deliverance, I could tell this would take a while, and there were going to be some manifestations along the way. A lot of times in these situations the manifestations that appear are not necessarily to do with the person but are more about a show to distract the person who is there to facilitate the deliverance. This process was about four hours, which is longer than I would normally go in one session, but the demons were working really hard to stay. The further we progressed, the more resistant they were to my commands. Ultimately if the person is giving me this authority and wants this to happen then the demons must obey the authority I have in Jesus. The same authority we all have. However, in this particular case, they were stalling. The enemy was intending to use manifestations to scare me or deceive me into thinking I couldn't make them leave. They tried several manifestations like having her head roll around and making her face contort to see if that would make me freak out because then they can gain some ground. As long as the person isn't being harmed, I don't react to anything they are doing. The name calling doesn't matter to me; the evil words don't matter to me; they hold no power or authority. So, I keep going with my commands for them to leave. They will try to have conversation, which is intended to make me lose focus on my agenda to evict them.

Whether the enemy is using tactics that are subtle or bold, we can't lose our focus. They will work as hard as they need to because they know if they can get us distracted one time, they can build on breaking us down in our relationship and in our time with the Lord.

So how do we overcome these attempts at our time and attention? First let's go back to see who the demon of distraction works with and how that plays on our emotions.

When we are feeling: frustration, indifference,

When we are experiencing: forgetfulness, confusion, procrastination, and restlessness

Those demons are working to make us feel vulnerable. The thing about our feelings is that we can't always trust our own feelings. How many times have you had your feelings hurt only to later find out you misunderstood something someone said. Our feelings are not always the best judge of a situation, so we need to be aware that our feelings can distract us from the Lord. Someone asked me last night in a discussion about the essentialness of daily prayer, "What do I do if I don't feel like praying?" My response is simple, you pray anyway, even if it's just saying "Jesus, Jesus, Jesus " over and over again. Don't let feelings override your actions because they will distract you and confuse your purpose and direction.

To overcome distraction, be mindful of your feelings directing your actions. We also need to be honest about our time management and how much time we are spending with the Lord. Look back at the last week and see where you intended to spend time with the Lord and evaluate it by activity, church, prayer, bible study, and reading the bible. Break it all out so you can see the patterns develop. Document how or why you were distracted and didn't do what you had planned. Then decide how you will correct it. We need to be intentional about what we do and being accountable if we have a problem with distractions.

If we look at Jesus as an example, we will have a better understanding of how to improve our own lives. Jesus frequently stepped away from everyone and had his alone time with His Father. That was a necessity in His life and if it was necessary for the Jesus then we are no exception and should model what worked for Him in our own lives.

Chapter 23

Discouragement

To fully understand the Spirit of Discouragement, we need to know specifically how the Spirit of Discouragement works and how we not only allow it, but nurture it in the way we respond.

Let's get to know the Spirit of Discouragement a bit before we talk about how we allow it and nurture it. The Spirit of Discouragement is extremely powerful. There are three main reasons why Discouragement is so powerful.

First, the Spirit of Discouragement enters our life slowly, quietly, and in ways we don't readily recognize. Of course, there are times when it comes in with a bang, usually by someone with little understanding and discernment of our situation. Those people tend to be negative and discouraging everywhere they go, and that is precisely what we are not wanting to replicate. What we are talking about here is how little seeds of discouragement, weeds actually, are planted and we don't recognize them as weeds, so we allow them to grow. We don't rebuke it or turn to the Lord in trust and faith, or even ask for an increase in trust and faith in our circumstances. Instead, we let that weed grow. Some weeds can even look pretty convincingly like they belong in our cultivated garden. When we don't exercise discernment and work with the Holy Spirit, we don't recognize it for what it is. In the natural, Google makes it easy for us to see a plant growing. We can take a picture and Google will identify it for us and let us know if it is friend or foe to our garden. I say garden; I don't have a garden. I have tried. I can grow tomatoes, but I tried to grow strawberries and onions, and I was diligently caring for the soil only to later realize my dogs ate up all of my precious seedlings except for the tomatoes. If my garden had been in the spirit realm, I could have used discernment to see the enemy to my garden, my dogs, had eaten everything up before I was even able to cultivate a single strawberry. Jesus dealt with this same issue and showed us how to deal with it. Matthew 21, gives us the story starting with verse 18, "*Early in the morning, as Jesus was on his way back to the city, he was hungry. Seeing a fig tree by the road, he went up to it but found nothing on it except leaves. Then he said to it, "May you never bear fruit again!" Immediately the tree withered. When the disciples saw this, they were amazed. "How did the fig tree wither so quickly?" they asked. Jesus replied, "Truly I tell you, if you have faith and do not doubt, not only can you do what was done to the fig tree, but also you can say to this mountain, 'Go, throw yourself into the sea,' and it will be done. If you believe, you will receive whatever you ask for in prayer."*

Most people look at that story for the "ask" portion, for prayer, but I want to talk about the tree. This fig tree was on the side of the road on the way into Jerusalem. This road was not new to Jesus, as He spent much of his time in this area. This tree gave the appearance to Jesus from some distance that it was mature enough to bear fruit so we can infer from that it was not a little seedling, or a newly planted sapling. The tree had been there for a while. Fig trees are very good-looking trees. My neighbor behind me has one so

I look at it every day and watch their figs ripen. I saw them in Israel, they provide good shade in the heat because they are very full, and the leaves are huge compared to many other trees. Genesis 3:7 tells us Adam and Eve sewed together fig leaves for covering once they realized they were naked. Back to my point. Jesus and His disciples, not to mention everyone else in that area, undoubtedly walked past this tree on more than one occasion, but it wasn't until Jesus decided to harvest the fruit of this tree did He see that there was nothing to harvest. The tree was in the midst of everyone, it grew, it was recognized for what it appeared to be, but it was not what it appeared to be. As a result, Jesus did not hesitate to dispense the fig tree. Likewise, we need to see the people around us, the words used over us and with us, the activities that we are doing and not doing for what they are to us in our walk with the Lord. When someone or something is a discouragement, call it out for what it is and do not let it hinder your relationship with the Lord. Discernment is needed here in order to not let your own desires trump what the Lord is doing in your life. If someone is offering you godly wisdom, listen to them and ask the Lord about it. Discernment reveals the difference between godly wisdom to give you guidance and discouragement meant to send you down a path of doubt and loss.

The second reason Discouragement is so powerful is because it can work with any demon grouping. If you remember from Chapter 6 where I discussed specific demons and groupings, we went over how and why certain demons work well together. Some demons are just a more natural fit with others in their attempts to lead us to destruction. The thing with discouragement is that it is a bit like vanilla. Vanilla pairs well with nearly everything. You can use vanilla in drinks of all kinds, hot, cold, alcoholic, since it blends well and enhances other flavors. It works well with fruits, both citrus and berries. I don't know of any herb or spice that can't combine with vanilla. Vanilla can be sweet or savory. It works in meat sauces, and in marinades. We use it for soap, perfume, air freshener. Vanilla is everywhere. Real vanilla is very expensive. Real vanilla costs almost as much as silver per ounce. Now let's compare vanilla to discouragement. Is there any area in your life you can think of that is completely immune to discouragement? I can't think of any areas which are immune. Our careers, our family life, our marriages, our prayer life, our friendships, our finances, our businesses - all of it and more are all prone to have some aspect that we can feel discouraged by. Like vanilla, discouragement comes with a cost, and it is expensive. If we allow discouragement to flavor any area of our lives, it can be hard to get it out. I love vanilla, but if it were causing problems in my life, it would be down the drain in my house. We cannot afford to allow our minds or our hearts to be flavored with discouragement. If you already have challenges in your life, look to root out the discouragement and even find out where it entered your life. Seek out that source so you can block it the next time. If you have someone in your life who continually brings you discouragement, have a conversation with that person about it and explain how it is affecting you, and let them know you cannot allow that to continue in your life. They either need to change how they are speaking into your life, or you need to change what you are allowing in your life through them. If you are watching the news and find that you are reacting in a way that is causing you to behave negatively, then you need to reevaluate what news you are watching. We need to be mindful of where we have allowed discouragement to grow because it can be a connector between other issues. If you have financial challenges right now, discouragement can attach to that challenge and pull

222

together other aspects in your life. Before you know it, you are not only challenged with finances, but other areas as well because you sowed into the discouragement in your finances and allowed it to grow into other areas that weren't even a challenge for you.

The third reason discouragement is so powerful if we allow it, is that it can and will keep you from moving forward with the Lord. The whole point, the whole objective of the Spirit of Discouragement is to keep you from victory. We can have victory in every area of our life with the Lord, but if Discouragement can keep you from taking ahold of that victory, then it is fulfilling its role in Satan's kingdom. I guarantee you other demons see Discouragement and welcome him in because they know they will increase their score with an assist from Discouragement. We can't have victory if we keep losing over and over to Discouragement.

Let me tell you a story about fighting Discouragement.

This story began in August of 2022. My husband and I had just returned from exploring ancient ruins in Turkey, and he had to go to Japan for two or three weeks for work. He's in the military and there were several of the men from my husband's unit on this trip. On one of the Sundays, August 7th, to be exact, about ten guys set out from the base, drove the hour and a half to Mt Fuji with the intent of spending the day climbing Mt Fuji. For the average fit person, it should take about 6 hours to ascend and then roughly the same to descend. Mt Fuji is the highest mountain in Japan, at 12,388 feet and 3 inches. Mt Everest is a bit over 29,000 feet to give you some perspective on size. Mt Fuji is a pretty good size mountain.

Having just come back from Turkey, my husband and I had been doing some hiking, about ten miles a day, but he wasn't fully prepared for Fuji. A lot of times in our lives we are not fully prepared for what is ahead of us, and it's how we manage and navigate our circumstances that builds us or tears us down.

As the men arrived, they all knew they needed to meet back by 6pm. The gates to the mountain close at 6. The group of ten divide into smaller groups. My husband and two other men stay together. My husband is in his fifties, one of the men with him is in his twenties, and one is in his early thirties. Periodically I would get updates, my husband is like a cheer leader, and the number of pictures he was taking was pretty amazing. He is both the videographer and the photographer on all of our trips for our YouTube Channel, so he is in his element. He is with his men, doing something he was so excited to do. I'm sure he never imagined himself climbing Mt Fuji. For him it was a once in a lifetime event. As he progressed up the mountain, I watched using the GPS in our phones. The service was occasionally spotty, but I was able to keep pretty good track of him. His spirits were high, he was in his element. I shared pictures of his movement with one of my sons. My second son, Bryce, is an avid outdoorsman. He is one of those extreme sportsmen. He was so excited getting the updates, and he admitted how jealous he was that he wasn't with him. As the day progressed, I could sense changes in my husband's spirit.

I am having Don share the remaining story in his own words. He will be able to share from his perspective and give you a better understanding of the Discouragement he was facing that day. He started out so happy, but circumstances changed, and it became one of his most challenging days.

Don's story:

I'm at Mt Fuji. I never expected to be there. The view was amazing. I am with some guys from work I really like. I am outside, and I love being outside. As a kid, I loved hiking. To be able to go up on this mountain, I was excited from the beginning.

Unfortunately, we didn't get to eat before we left, and there was no place to buy breakfast before our early start. So, we already started out not fully prepared, and we knew better. We were able to rent the climbing gear, so we did have that, and I had a few snacks packed away in my bag. We had water and oxygen bottles. We were excited, committed, motivated to climb Mt Fuji. We started the climb, three of us together, and the others went on ahead of us. The view of Mt Fuji and the surrounding area was breathtaking. After a couple of hours into our climb, I started feeling a sharp pain in my knees. I tried to hide the pain and push through, but after a while I knew I had to let the guys know I was experiencing pain in my knees and needed to slow down. I realized that taking shorter steps was less painful. So, to remind myself to take shorter steps I used a two-word phrase to shorten my steps. I don't remember what the phrase was; it was like "slow and steady." I initially started feeling discouraged because I knew my pace was slowing the two other guys down, and we still had quite a ways to go for the summit. I felt like I was interfering in their progress and opportunity to reach the summit. They committed to staying with me, and we continued to climb. About an hour later, one of the guys with me injured his knee. In my mind, I felt he got injured having to change his pace for me. At this point, we are only about halfway up, but we decided together we are going to make it to the top whether we have to crawl, low crawl, whatever we had to do we didn't care; we were going to make it to the top. Even though two of us were both in pain, we pushed on. The terrain was different at times, sometimes steps, boulders, flat surfaces, steep angles, loose soil, but we kept pushing forward. Before you climb, you have the opportunity to buy a staff or a short stick; I bought a staff. As you climb, and at each station on the way up the mountain, you can stop and pay to have a wood burn mark in your staff. We would stop and get our marks giving us a few moments to rest and regroup. About three quarters of the way up, I walked past the station and turned right to look at the next section up toward the next station. The terrain was really rough and rocky, and I almost cried because it didn't look enjoyable because of the pain in my knees. We regrouped in front of the station; we talked about our options, the time, and we knew we were not going to make it to the top with the time we had left. We had to make a decision, and we decided to hit the escape trail for the descent. It was crushing to know we had to do that; we wanted to make it to the top. As we began the descent path, about twenty minutes in, two other guys in our group heard about my buddy's injury, and they changed their course and began the descent to administer first aid to his knee. One of the guys was a former navy corpsman, so he was a trained medic. While the corpsman was administering first aid, a second guy went down the mountain and let the mountain staff know we needed attention and arranged for us to get a ride down the mountain. We had to be down to the starting point at the foot of Mt Fuji by 6 pm in order to catch the bus, and the mountain staff assisting us assured us we would make it in time. At first, they could only accommodate with assistance down the mountain. So, the group, which was now four of us, was separated. Eventually everyone made it back down, and we were all back together. My buddy and I were in pain, knees were swelling, but we had to keep walking. Although we were so happy we were now at the bottom of the mountain, we still had to walk a half mile to get to the busses where the gate is located. We walked, but unfortunately did not arrive at the gate until 6:07, and the gate was closed and park staff would not allow us to leave the park. The rest of our group was on the other side of the gate with our bus. We did all we could to try to persuade them to let us out but it was not happening. We were now locked into the Mt Fuji visitor center until the next morning. There was no restaurant, nowhere to eat, no services; they had a lodge, but it closed at 6:30 and it was nowhere near the gate. So, off we went and made our way to the lodge. There are 4 of us in total: me, my two buddies and the medic. They had a room available, so we did get a room. It was one room for the four of us, and it was $300 cash. We scraped together the cash between the four of us for a room which consisted of four walls, a carpeted floor, 4 cot mattresses, no bathroom, no shower and a mural of Mt Fuji that was about 7 ft by 14 feet. As far as provisions, we had what we had been carrying with us all day, which between the four of us consisted of an apple, a couple of protein bars, a granola bar and water. It was hot and muggy. We opened the window for a draft only to be met with the scent of a sewer so we had to close the window. The level of discouragement was pretty high. We were all pretty discouraged. We were supposed to be at work the next day and we were stuck on Mt Fuji feeling defeated, trapped, like prisoners of the mountain.

The next morning, when we woke up, our spirits were a little lifted having rested; and the sun was shining, we decided to enjoy the views. We were told when we got the room we would get a free breakfast, and we were excited about getting a free breakfast. We were all packed up and set and ready to go for breakfast. We were so looking forward to sitting down having a meal. We didn't know what it was going to be, but we were looking forward to it. We soon found out that our free breakfast was a vending machine that we had to pay for, there was no way it was free. Once we found out about the vending machines, we were so deflated. We were not going to pay for breakfast. That was not going to happen. So, we gathered our stuff up, went outside, in front of the lodge and we were talking, voicing our disgruntledness. There were a few small vendors out front, and one kind Japanese lady gestured to us and gave us a puffy dough with meat in it. A steamed meat bun. I was so joyful; we hadn't eaten, we were so happy.

As we ate and got something in our belly, we then were able to take a moment and reflect on what we had been through. We were thankful that it was daytime, and we could enjoy the scenery and the drive back to base. We were still sore; we knew we needed to go the doctor for our injuries and weren't sure what they were going to say, but we were thankful for the opportunity to climb Mt Fuji and experience something most people aren't able to do.

I remember that being a difficult day for Don. It felt like every time we communicated, which wasn't much as the day progressed because he didn't have a charger, Don was just getting more and more discouraged and I knew it was a hard day. It was how he managed the challenges and accepted that his desire, his expectation, his hope to reach the summit was not going to happen that speaks of who he is as a man. He didn't mention it, but I know he was praying through that situation and praying with the guys he was with even though none of them were Christian.

Now the story doesn't end there. The story ended exactly a year later. My son, Bryce, the extreme sportsman, is also in the military. In November of 2022, he was sent to Japan. About a month before he was scheduled to come home, he was invited by some guys to go climb Mt Fuji. Bryce and the guys took a 3-hour train ride from the base to Mt Fuji. Bryce didn't think he was going to get the opportunity to go to Mt Fuji, so he was excited. He didn't really even know the guys who invited him, but they knew he would enjoy it, so they asked him to join. Bryce didn't prepare for it either since he was asked last minute. He actually did the climb in vans, street shoes, a pair of shorts and a t-shirt. He too bought a stick to have the wood burn stamp at the various mountain stations. He saw my husband's stick before he left for Japan and thought it was pretty cool, I think he said "sick" actually, to have as a keepsake. Bryce is a pretty friendly guy; he is extremely fit and once they arrived, he came up with a plan for how quickly he wanted to make the ascent. He was ahead of the group he traveled with and met people all along the way. He stopped at the stations and got his wood burn stamps as my husband did. At one point, he met two Americans, also military guys and was chatting with them. They asked him something about his climb since he was alone, and he explained he was with a group, but he was trying to make the ascent within a certain timeframe. Once they realized what he was doing, they quickly realized that talking to them was slowing him down. They encouraged him to get on and not let them interfere. At one station he was having trouble communicating with a vendor, and a Japanese woman helped him out. Then they chatted a bit as she explained some things to him about the culture and tradition of Mt Fuji. Bryce then continued on his way and reached the summit; he reached it in 2 hours and 45 minutes. On his way down, the terrain was rough and because he was in vans, he slipped and cut open his hand pretty badly. Along the way he ran into the same Japanese woman he had chatted with previously, and she gave him first aid. She insisted, which was incredibly kind. Bryce was very excited that this one thing he was so happy my husband was able to do - and which he too had wanted to do, he was actually able to do just weeks before he was to leave Japan. We picked Bryce up from the airport in San Diego and he apologized that he did not buy gifts for us. He said "Actually, I did buy one gift," but he wanted to make sure I knew he wasn't playing favorites. While at Fuji, he bought an additional walking stick and had it stamped with the 4 additional stops Don could not achieve when he was at Fuji.

Even though Don could not complete the ascent, the Lord still gave him the gift of the walking stick through

Bryce. Don was so touched that Bryce would think to do that for him.

When you are having your Fuji day, what kind of person are you going to be? Are you going to stand by someone else when they are struggling even when you are struggling? Are you going to encourage someone to keep going and move ahead so they can achieve a goal like those men did for Bryce? Instead of being jealous or petty when he explained he was trying to achieve the ascent in an incredibly fast pace, they supported him, and they didn't even know him. Are you going to be like the Japanese woman and help someone out when they are in need? How are you going to react when you are in pain, and you realize you are not leaving the mountain tonight? When you have had a hard day and you have very limited resources, what will you turn to God with? Anger? Frustration? All of the things we encounter in our lives provide an opportunity for discouragement. It is how we allow that opportunity to grow – or not grow - in our lives that determines how deep our relationship with the Lord will become.

James tells us this, 1: 2-8 *"Consider it pure joy, my brothers and sisters, whenever you face trials of many kinds, because you know that the testing of your faith produces perseverance. Let perseverance finish its work so that you may be mature and complete, not lacking anything. If any of you lacks wisdom, you should ask God, who gives generously to all without finding fault, and it will be given to you. But when you ask, you must believe and not doubt, because the one who doubts is like a wave of the sea, blown and tossed by the wind. That person should not expect to receive anything from the Lord. Such a person is double-minded and unstable in all they do."*

231

Think of discouragement like your Mt Fuji. Some days your discouragement may be like Don's climb: long, difficult, painful and nothing like you were expecting. Some days it may be like Bryce's, and you may be having a great day, but on your way down you get cut up when you slip on some jagged rocks. They were on the same path, completely different days. Neither allowed discouragement to take them out. Decide how you will handle your Mt Fuji. Stay committed to overcoming Discouragement, and let it draw you closer to the Lord with every step.

Chapter 24

Disbelief and Disillusionment

I say periodically throughout our time together here that not all bad things that happen are Satan and his demons at work against us. Many times, it is, and we want to be knowledgeable and educated on how Satan operates so we can conquer him, and render his tactics no longer effective. For now, we need to address something that has permeated Christianity and not only affects us in our daily lives but can limit us in our relationship with the Lord going forward.

Let's first start off addressing disbelief and disillusionment. There are multiple ways we let these two states of being take over our life and our circumstances, and we need to uproot some misconceptions and the lies that allow these two to operate.

First off, I want you to think about a time when you made a judgment call and you were just flat out wrong, or someone made a judgment call about you that was just flat out wrong. Think of something. Got one? Okay, I will tell you mine for this week. Friday I was called a heretic. Now not just a regular old heretic, there was some pretty harsh name calling that went along with that rebuke from a Christian man because I believe in the spiritual gifts - the spiritual gifts that Paul lists in 1 Corinthians 12. Now I know this guy is completely wrong and one day he will have to answer for his words. I don't care about him. What I do care about is the effect his words had on the man who originally asked the question I was answering. The ripple effect of the ignorant man can have a lasting effect. It can shape the mind of others who are on the fence. The ignorant man was relentless in going after anyone who had beliefs that were different from his, and he became very ugly about it. It's as if he was throwing a tantrum to get people to listen to him and not think for themselves. To him, only his words mattered. He was creating an atmosphere for disbelief in the spiritual gifts of the Bible.

Now let's talk about a time when something just wasn't going your way and you were really struggling. Have one? I am going to share an example of a man who is currently blaming God for bad things happening in his life. This is a man who says he was healthy and lived a healthy lifestyle. I have no way to deny or confirm this. He is a middle-aged man, and he had a heart attack and a stroke. As a result, he has lost his job, his girlfriend, his confidence, and he is unable to spend time in the gym the way he used to and has become depressed. He is convinced that God did this to him and that instead of taking his life from the heart attack and stroke, God kept him alive for the purpose of torturing him.

Considering those two situations, they both have one thing in common. They both involve someone who is putting himself at the center of the situation. The first situation involves how disbelief is perpetuated by someone who will not allow people to believe what the Bible says if it disagrees with what they think the Bible says. He attacks and tries to force himself to convince others - which then impacts others who are attempting to learn and trying to understand. The second situation involves a man who is disillusioned into thinking that God would do something evil, which is blasphemy and a lie.

Blaming God is very common and a very manmade idea, not always from Satan. Satan will be more than happy to exploit that and take advantage of it, but by and large when we carry disbelief and disillusionment in our lives, we create it in our thoughts and in our words and our actions. But the question is why? No one is happy in disbelief or functioning in disillusionment so why do we do it? Why do we fight God in this way?

The answer is pretty straightforward. It stems from disobedience or ego. This goes back to what we read about in Deuteronomy 28 regarding Blessings and Curses, but we need to talk about how we direct this in our lives. We must be willing to self-identify when we are growing in disbelief and disillusionment and thereby building problems against ourselves.

No one who truly knows Jesus would ever say that God spared their life just to torture them. You cannot read the Bible and come to that conclusion; it is illogical, unbiblical and a complete and utter lie. If you aren't reading the Bible, you can't know who God is, or how He works. If we don't know who God is, then how can we understand anything about how He wants to work in our lives. If we can't understand anything He wants to do in our lives, then we clearly don't have a relationship with Him because He will spend time guiding you and explaining to you His best in your life if invited to.

Those who are disillusioned and want to blame God don't acknowledge that they are looking for ways, for resolutions, and for answers outside of the Word. When we function in disbelief and disillusionment because we are unwilling to seek the Lord, we have created our own downfall.

When we are in disbelief and disillusionment, we are also housing distrust. There's a selfishness we carry which manifests in discontentment and indifference to seeking God - truly seeking Him through prayer and His Word. We want to do things our own way and not allow God to correct us nor direct us to make better choices, provide understanding to foster better decisions. We don't want to be disciplined; we don't want anyone calling out our dirty laundry. We aren't willing to discipline ourselves to change.

Let's look at how Jesus handled a woman who had dirty laundry and when He called her on it, she reacted. In John 4, Jesus meets a Samaritan woman. Jews and Samaritans at this time did not mingle. There was a distrust and a hatred for each other. Samaritans were a culture that originated out of the Israelites, the northern kingdom. Each group believes themselves to be members of the true religion of ancient Israel. That the other has been diluted or contaminated might be a better description of their prejudice. Jesus meets this woman getting water from the well because that was a typical responsibility of the women of the day. He asks for water; He tells her He is the living water and then He also tells her about her life and essentially airs her dirty laundry. The fact that she was alone, not accompanied by other women in the village is a hint to her exclusion in her own community due to her sin. Her reaction is not one we see today. Her ego did not get in her way. She did not allow disbelief to enter her heart and she was certainly not disillusioned by what He has said or done anywhere else because she didn't even know who He was. She knew the truth was in Him and therefore, believed in Him.

Jesus was able to move in her heart and guide her to change her life and her response was to run and tell the rest of the village what just happened. She focused on Him, not herself, and she acted in faith by running to get the others so they too could benefit from hearing what he had to say.

So why are we talking about this? I'm going to ask you to do something this week. Sit down and take an inventory. This is just between you and the Lord so be open. Take an inventory of areas in your life where you have exhibited great belief. Consider the areas where you have excelled in faith.

Then I want you to take an inventory of areas in your relationship with the Lord where you have exhibited disbelief and disillusionment. Include times you have felt He wasn't answering your prayers, turned His back on you or didn't give you the outcome you thought you should have received. Again, this is just between you and Him so be honest.

After you have both of these lists completed, you are going to go back and evaluate these lists. What can you count as favor and blessing you have received because of your belief and faith? What did you do to foster that belief and faith? What actions did you take? Now look at the disbelief list and list what you did to foster disbelief. What actions did you take? What thoughts did you allow? Did you talk to someone who helped build your faith or build your disbelief? Compare these two lists and look at your differences.

What I have seen in working with people over the years is that when they hit a period of disbelief, they quit seeking and building their relationship with the Lord and instead direct their frustrations at God. Those disbeliefs will grow. Many times, the feeling associated with disbeliefs will grow faster than how we feel when we are operating in faith and belief that God is truly working on our behalf.

We have the greatest ability to be our own unseen enemy, and as much as we need to conquer Satan, we need to conquer the pieces of ourselves that allow disobedience, disbelief, disillusionment, indifference, distrust, selfishness to grow.

Go read John 4 and ask yourself, are you going to be like the Samaritan woman or are you going to just get your water and go home?

Part Four:

Forging Our Weapons

Chapter 25

Overcoming weaknesses and temptations

Before we begin, we must understand that not all weaknesses are the works of Satan. Not all temptations are a source from the demonic. There are also times when our weaknesses are opened up, and we feel like a wound torn open. Through those weaknesses, God is going to then come beside us, encourage us, and build us up in Him by having us walk through our weaknesses with Him. We need to understand and believe in Him first before we start talking about the temptations the enemy brings. We shouldn't always assume that everything that hits our weakness is from the enemy. Once we acknowledge that, then we can move on to address what the enemy is actually attempting to do to us.

Let's start with defining weakness and temptation.

The definition of weakness is the state or condition of lacking strength.

The definition of temptation is the desire to do something, especially something wrong or unwise.

The demons we see when dealing with our weaknesses and temptations are endless because it is such a personal matter. For some it will be doubt or fear, but for others lust or gluttony - the list goes on. Our discussion here isn't about a specific demon but rather the process behind how they work and how we need to respond. Our response is what defines our beliefs. Our beliefs are what define us ultimately. Let me explain.

There are times when we will be tempted in areas that aren't actually our weakness, but the enemy thinks we can be swayed to make the wrong choice because of our circumstances. It is during those moments when we can be manipulated to come into agreement with the enemy. Recognition that manipulation of the enemy is a lie and is not who we are in alignment with the Lord's plan in our lives, is imperative. Let me give you an example. This past week I got a call, about 9:30 at night from a friend of mine. I happen to be a huge animal lover. In my life I have had over a couple of hundred animals easily between pets, fosters, and they are all types: lizards, snakes, turtles, dogs, cats, rabbits, guinea pig, hamster, fish, and, of course, all the parrots I have now. So, if you ever call me about an animal, I am going to listen. This particular call from my friend was about their cat, Pumpkin. I didn't ask Pumpkin's permission to use her name, but I think she will still be able to maintain her anonymity. Anyhow, Pumpkin had some young kittens to take care of but on this particular night, Pumpkin, who is an indoor cat, was nowhere to be found. We have coyotes that come into our neighborhoods at night in this area so you always have to be careful around here even with larger dogs. One night I was walking with two dogs and we came up on a pack of five coyotes which was pretty terrifying. Anyway, back to the Pumpkin predicament. Now you can understand why the family was pretty anxious and they asked for prayer. We put a prayer game plan together and agreed to keep in touch until she returned. Our pets can create a huge weakness for all of us. For everyone I know, their pet is their family. So, this prayer plan was a good plan, but it did involve faith on the part of the family that what we were asking of God, He would fulfill. No matter how the situation looked, their faith in Him had to remain solid. In our prayer plan, we were asking God to have Pumpkin return that night. I like to be specific in my prayer requests, so we asked for it to happen that night in part because of the kittens. I checked in with them at 10:15, nothing yet. I'll be honest with you, guys, I was asking the Lord to show up BIG on this one. I even went so far as to say, Lord, if something has happened to that cat, then I need that cat to raise up from the dead and get back to that house tonight. Sounds silly, but if Pumpkin were yours that's what you would want, so I asked. This was at a time her when kids were learning the importance of faith so asking for the unusual to me is reasonable. So, where is the temptation or the weakness in this? Well, the faith was needed was where a weakness could have been exploited by the enemy to get any one of the family members to be discouraged and say "she's gone, she's never coming back." If the family had been weak in those moments and had come into alignment with the enemy in any declaration other than what they are asking the Lord for, Pumpkin's story could have had a sad ending. Our words matter. Would you like to know how Pumpkin's story ended? Well as it was nearing midnight the family ended their search of the neighborhood and headed home. They were sad to give up the search, but they had to go back home to take care of the kittens. Within minutes of their return, one of the daughters took one last look in the backyard through the sliding glass door, and all of a sudden, Pumpkin appeared in their backyard and, of course, the family was elated.

We are not defined by our weaknesses. We are more defined by our response in the moment of weakness and by how we respond and react based on what we believe. We must understand we have a "standing" in the Lord. What do I mean by that? When I was in law school, one of the first concepts we learned was legal "standing."

"In simple terms, the courts use the term "standing" to ask, "Does this party have a 'dog in this fight?'" Standing limits or allows participation in lawsuits by asking whether the person(s) bringing a lawsuit, or defending one, (you will often hear of groups adding in a legal positioning in cases that affect a class of people) but that person or group has enough cause to "stand" before the court and advocate, since not anyone can go to court for any reason."

As a believer, our "standing" is in the Lord. Our ability to "stand" before the Lord and contend for someone or something in our prayers is given to us by our accepting Jesus as our Savior. Without that "standing," we will have a hard time defending ourselves against enemy attacks because we won't have the power and authority of Jesus. Our "standing" is our strength and our shield as the Psalmist says in Psalms 28:7. Pumpkin's family knew their "standing," and they did not waiver.

Let's talk about "standing" a little more. Our "standing" is our Truth. Our "standing" will not change once we have it. It will never fluctuate. Our feelings, on the other hand, will fluctuate and we cannot allow our feelings and emotions to rule our lives. The enemy will prey on our weaknesses, so we need to prevent the enemy from having an influence in our feelings or emotions. If we feel our emotions wavering, we need to rebuke, and our response is to declare our standing. There will be times, however, when the Lord sees a situation coming, and will intercede for us because of our standing. I'll explain that a little more in a minute, but first I want to hit a few points.

Demons are witnesses to our lives in the same way as angels are witnesses. Police psychics or mediums can help solve crimes because demons were present when these horrible events took place; they know what happened, and they simply tell the medium. It's not rocket science. It is wrong to communicate with demons that way, but rocket science it is not.

Knowing that demons are witnesses to our lives is important. Peter tells us in 1 Peter 5:8, *"Be alert and of sober mind. Your enemy the devil prowls around like a roaring lion looking for someone to devour."* They are like those coyotes I referenced earlier. Let me tell you about that night. I was out on a walk. It was evening about 8:30, a Saturday night actually, and it was already dark. The strip of road I was on was outside of my neighborhood, and the streetlight in that stretch of the road was out. The next streetlight was over a quarter a mile away. One of my dogs was a little guy, maybe twelve pounds, his name was Blackie. One of the kids named him because well, he was black. Not terribly creative but he didn't seem to mind. The other dog was a border collie mix, so mediumish size, maybe forty-five to fifty pounds at the most. His name was Shadow because he followed me everywhere and he was black. Again, not overly creative on our part. The neighborhood where we lived was very safe so I only had a cell phone on me. It was pitch black in this area and on one side of me were a few baseball fields and on the other side were wild lands. The coyotes lived in the wild lands, which consisted of several. Coyotes usually, I hate to say it, but coyotes were usually well fed from the wild rabbits. I had never walked here at this time before and never did it again. I did notice a few times as we were walking along, that Blackie stopped and looked behind. Shadow was just focused on going straight ahead, not stopping. As we walked, all of a sudden, there was something white about twenty feet away in the middle of the street walking with its head down and turned toward me, but his body was sideways. I have seen coyotes since I was a kid, and they are usually about the same size as Shadow, but this one was HUGE; it looked like a wolf. They are also usually tan, but this thing was bright white, like he was glowing, a pearly translucent fog surrounding him. It was crazy to see. Then I realized there were four more and they were circling me, and the circle was getting smaller. I called home, but no one answered. Four people were home and not one person answered. I was about half mile from my house if I were to turn back. I wasn't sure what to do, but I did pick up Blackie, and at that point Shadow was doing his best menacing behavior, but we were not going to be able to withstand five of them on our own.

That's how an attack can be from demons who see us in a weak moment. The temptation method the coyotes used was entice me to do something unwise out of fear while being distracted. By having the white one in front of me, I would be distracted and too fearful with that one to not notice when one or two of the others would come at me from behind or the side. They will snatch a dog out of your hands by the way, so Blackie was far from safe just because I was holding him. I am only 5'1" so all they had to do was grab him by the tail or his neck. I would love to tell you I took authority over those coyotes and held them back with my hand like Moses did the Red Sea, but my story is a little less dramatic. We decided our best move was to get to the light ahead, and so we became as menacing as we could, loud and aggressive so we could keep moving and try to confuse them into thinking twice about getting closer. Not exactly my most heroic moment, but it worked, and someone finally answered the phone, and they all came to pick us up with the car. I have zero doubt it was the Holy Spirit who made that coyote glow, or I would not have seen it until it was too late and Blackie would have been no more and most likely the same with Shadow. Shadow, however, lived to a ripe old age of nineteen and Blackie passed in my arms about eight years later. What I want to point out is that I had no idea those coyotes were there, but the Holy Spirit did. The Holy Spirit was there to reveal the danger in a glowing white way so I could not miss so I did not have to withstand an attack. I had "standing." I was at a weak point, but the Holy Spirit was there before I even knew I was in danger.

When Jesus spent His time in the wilderness for forty days and forty nights, Satan did his best to tempt Jesus by preying on his human weakness and vulnerabilities. You can read about this in Matthew 4. Jesus knew His "standing" in His Father and withstood everything the enemy attempted by responding with the Word. If I had not eaten for forty days, I hope I would be that able minded, but I also know that because of my "standing" the Lord will help me in those moments. No matter how weak we are, how much the temptation, we can withstand through our "standing" in Him and for Him and through Him. Luke puts it so eloquently in Acts 17:38, *"For in Him we live, and move, and have our being;"* When I get to heaven I want to spend some time with Luke. I think he is overlooked. I overlooked him myself for years because he wasn't one of the original ones, no one knows for certain where he was during the time when Jesus was here, but he certainly devoted his life to being an attentive onlooker, scribe and servant for the Lord. When you realize that, what Luke did was entirely for our benefit, you can't help but respect and admire him.

So, what do I want you to take away from this? I want you to be able to face any temptation, any weakness with the strength of your "standing." When you know, truly know you have "standing" and that your "standing" is what will carry you through anything in your life, you will stand a little taller, walk a little surer. I don't know if surer is a word, but it is for today! The enemy knows you have "standing," so you should too. Standing works in the courts of this world, and it certainly works in the courts of heaven. The accuser, our enemy, doesn't want you to understand this concept. If you don't understand it or chose to deny it, then how can you get to a place where Jesus is your intercessor, where the Holy Spirit is your comforter, where you can know the truth and say in all certainty what Paul reveals to us in Romans 8:31, *"what then shall we say to these things? If God is for us, who can be against us?"*

The next time you are weak, stand tall, and let your response reflect your "standing."

Chapter 26

5 Steps to Overcome a Spiritual Attack

Do you remember the last time you felt like you were under a spiritual attack where you just keep getting hit over and over no matter what you did? Well, you are not alone. We all have these times in our lives. While sometimes we are going through challenges that aren't necessarily a spiritual attack, these five steps we are going to discuss will serve you well and get you through your storm. No matter who you are, life is full of challenges, and we need to be armed and ready to take on those challenges so that we come out of them stronger, more resilient and better able to discern how the Lord is guiding us through it.

We know that 1 Peter 5:8 tells us *"Be alert and of sober mind. Your enemy the devil prowls around like a roaring lion looking for someone to devour."* When we are in the midst of an attack, it does feel like this, doesn't it? We sometimes let ourselves feel defeated when we keep getting hit with yet another thing. Let's look at what that scripture is telling us. We know the devil is around us, it may not be twenty-four hours a day, but we know there are times when he is working hard against us. Peter doesn't say when we are doing good things, or when a breakthrough is coming; there is no qualifier to when he prowls. He just prowls like a roaring lion, looking for someone to devour. Years ago, I used to be a member of the LA Zoo. I was a member before I even had kids because I just love animals. One of the benefits of being a member is that you get to get in earlier than non-members. So, I would intentionally plan my early entries to try to be at certain enclosures when the animals first came out. This one day, I wanted to be there for the lion. The lion enclosure is nowhere near the entrance, so I had to plan the route I was going to take, and I had to time it because it was too far to walk and be there in time to see him come out.

I remember that day, it was a sunny day, it was twenty-nine or thirty years ago, and I ran the path I had established was the best route. I ran through winding paths, up little hills, down little hills, up big hills, down big hills, by myself, to make my way to the last curve leading me to the lion enclosure. I arrived, out of breath, and made it to front and center of the enclosure where the lion would come out from the back enclosure. The front enclosure, sadly, is not very big, it's kind of pie shaped if you were to take one third of a pie, which can happen in my house with pumpkin pie, but I digress. The distance between me and the edge of where the lion can come out is maybe forty to fifty feet at most. The space that makes up those forty to fifty feet drops down like a moat, but there's no water there because we live in a desert. Anyhow, I was at the center of the enclosure facing the gate where the lion comes out just at the moment the lion was released and came out. He looked kind of angry or amped up, and he came out of that gate with a start and stepped right to the edge of the enclosure in front of me, stared straight at me and let out a roar I will never forget. I stood there, witnessing this beautiful lion with his mouth open, roar so loud the noise traveled across the 40-50 feet and enter my body, shaking me from head to toe. I was shook! I was also a little scared. I was thankful that lion presumably could not make the forty-to-fifty-foot leap across that enclosure to get to me because he truly looked like he wanted to let out some frustrations on me. When I read that scripture, like a roaring lion, I have that as my perspective. A roaring lion is terrifying without an enclosure to protect me.

As believers, I think at times we are too nonchalant about how we view a spiritual attack.

You often hear believers talk like this:

The enemy is really attacking me lately. Then someone responds with... well then you must be doing something right, or... then breakthrough must be right around the corner.

That may be true, but so what! How does that help us while we are in the midst of an attack? Don't we all hope we are doing something right or have a breakthrough coming? But what difference does it make? In our thought process we should not qualify the enemy attack with a Kingdom advance. The enemy should not have an open door to attack us. The scripture said *"Be alert and of sober mind"* We need to change the narrative and go on the offense as soon as we think we are under attack. If it turns out it wasn't a spiritual attack and is instead a consequence of a bad choice, then we have still trained ourselves on how to respond under all circumstances. We aren't going to train ourselves to sit and wait while we are in the storm. We are going to train ourselves to be forward advancing for the Kingdom working with God always, under all circumstances, no matter how we feel.

An enemy attack can be very simple or an attack can be very elaborate. Regardless of what type of attack you are experiencing, there are five steps we can follow to get us through the attack successfully and bring us closer to the Lord at the same time.

1.   Put everything in perspective:

When we are experiencing an attack or even if we aren't sure if it is an attack, but it feels like the world is against us, we need pull back from our circumstances and gain some perspective. As a believer, we have everything we need to overcome our circumstance. It can be easy to lose sight of that when we are in the midst of our difficulties, but no matter what the enemy attempts to do around us, we know what John 16:33 tells us, *"I have told you these things, so that in me you may have peace. In this world you will have trouble. But take heart! I have overcome the world."* This alone tells us we know our outcome, but we have to walk through some things to get there. In our walk we must start with putting everything in perspective, and these verses can help you do that. These are great verses to add to your scripture journal. This is why a scripture journal is so essential.

Psalm 46:10, *"Be still, and know that I am God. I will be exalted among the nations, I will be exalted in the earth!"*

Psalm 112:7, *"He is not afraid of bad news; his heart is firm, trusting in the Lord."*

Galatians 6:9, *"And let us not grow weary of doing good, for in due season we will reap, if we do not give up."*

Romans 8:28, *And we know that for those who love God all things work together for good, for those who are called according to his purpose.*

2.   Don't let the challenge be a distraction. Refocus:

Often times when we are facing an attack, it becomes all we think about. We almost wait for the next thing to happen. When we wait expectantly, we are coming into agreement with the enemy, and we must change that thought process. We can't continue to think of ourselves at the receiving end of whatever the enemy wants to throw at us. Instead, turn the situation around and start to take aim at the enemy tactics and don't just build your defense, which at times is all we think we can do. This is the time to go on the offense. Don't let the negative situation turn you into a weak and willing participant with the enemy. This can be really hard depending on what you are dealing with. Sometimes all we see is what is in front of us, but we must stop thinking just about what is in front of us if we are going to get through this with the Lord. I know people who faced with a difficulty, took time off work. When I asked what they did during that time, they did nothing. They wanted to just hide from the world, but that won't work. It only distracts us to go deeper into a hole that we need to walk away from and refocus our attention on the Lord.

Here are a few scriptures to get our hearts and minds refocused.

Colossians 3:2, *Set your minds on things that are above, not on things that are on earth.*

2 Corinthians 4:18, *As we look not to the things that are seen but to the things that are unseen. For the things that are seen are transient, but the things that are unseen are eternal.*

3.   Be more conscious of your time with the Lord:

When we are in the midst of a spiritual attack, we tend to let our usual routines fall by the wayside. Where we would normally pray, when things are really difficult, we don't pray the same. Our faith has dwindled. We have a desperation cry, or we turn on God and ask why, sometimes getting angry. We all have had moments where our emotions become that intense. Where we need to focus is in our time with the Lord. We need to make sure that we are not neglecting our time but instead investing our time with Him. We need to be more purposeful in our prayer time, add worship time into our daily schedule, even if it's only fifteen minutes. Read the Bible, and let Him speak to you. The more conscious we are of how we are spending our time and including the Lord in it, the easier it will be to overcome the attack. Using scripture positions us to send arrows right back at the enemy, and it will reduce the effectiveness of the attack and build you at the same time.

Here are some good ones to incorporate into your day:

Ephesians 6:18, *"And pray in the Spirit on all occasions with all kinds of prayers and requests. With this in mind, be alert and always keep on praying for all the Lord's people."*

1 Thessalonians 5:17, *"Pray without ceasing"*

Romans 10:17, *"So faith comes from hearing, and hearing through the word of Christ.*

4.   Slow down and seek the Lord on your decisions:

When we are in the midst of an attack, a lot of times we just want it to end as quickly as possible. Unfortunately, that can come at a steep cost if we are not careful. If we are not seeking the Lord and listening to Him on how to resolve a challenge, we could invite unexpected consequences we were not prepared for nor had the insight to understand would occur. We often try to use our earthly wisdom to deal with spiritual forces, and it doesn't work. The only way to overcome an enemy attack is with the Lord and following what He tells us to do and not do. He will give us the way we need which may not be the way we want, but it will be the way we need. We have to trust that His way is our way.

Matthew 7:7, *"Ask, and it will be given to you; seek, and you will find; knock, and it will be opened to you."*

Matthew 6:33, *"But seek first the kingdom of God and his righteousness, and all these things will be added to you."* (referring to provision)

Psalm 25:5, *"Lead me in your truth and teach me, for you are the God of my salvation; for you I wait all the day long."*

Psalm 27:14, *"Wait for the Lord; be strong, and let your heart take courage; wait for the Lord!"*

Psalm 62:5, *"For God alone, O my soul, wait in silence, for my hope is from him."*

5.   Stand firm in the truth of the Lord:

When things don't happen as quickly as we would like, humans have a tendency to try to hurry them along. Our culture is all about the hurrying of things along, what we can get or do faster gets us onto other things we can also do faster. The art of waiting is almost obsolete. Waiting with the Lord as He prepares you and strengthens you and shows

Conquering Our Unseen Enemies

you His way is actually exhilarating. When you can do this, you can forget about the difficulty and look forward to His outcome. Not a lot of people can do this, waiting can be challenging. I'm not going to deny that, but if you truly trust Him, you don't mind the wait. We can't expect God to be like a slot machine, we put something in and just push a button and something comes out. That's the way He is treated a lot. I would rather put all I have into Him, and then wait to see what He creates in and out of my circumstance.

I am in these last few weeks facing a spiritual attack. I haven't had one like this in a while. I wouldn't say I am enjoying it, but I am finding peace in it. I didn't actually count how many attacks I've had in this time period; it has been a series of attacks. It started as a cluster of attacks, a bunch of little attacks, then a week ago, some big things came at me. But the Lord has been with me and showing me how He is going to resolve things and how I can stand with Him in all that is happening.

These are some great scriptures to help you through this last step:

1 Corinthians 15:58, *"Therefore, my beloved brothers, be steadfast, immovable, always abounding in the work of the Lord, knowing that in the Lord your labor is not in vain."*

James 1:12, *"Blessed is the man who remains steadfast under trial, for when he has stood the test he will receive the crown of life, which God has promised to those who love him."*

Ephesians 6:10-18, *"Finally, be strong in the Lord and in the strength of his might. Put on the whole armor of God, that you may be able to stand against the schemes of the devil. For we do not wrestle against flesh and blood, but against the rulers, against the authorities, against the cosmic powers over this present darkness, against the spiritual forces of evil in the heavenly places. Therefore take up the whole armor of God, that you may be able to withstand in the evil day, and having done all, to stand firm. Stand therefore, having fastened on the belt of truth, and having put on the breastplate of righteousness, in place, and with your feet fitted with the readiness that comes from the gospel of peace. In addition to all this, take up the shield of faith, with which you can extinguish all the flaming arrows of the evil one. Take the helmet of salvation and the sword of the Spirit, which is the word of God."*

I want to end this discussion with a scripture because it really sums up everything we have discussed into one beautiful example of how He provides for us in everything:

James 1:2-4, *"Count it all joy, my brothers, when you meet trials of various kinds, for you know that the testing of your faith produces steadfastness. And let steadfastness have its full effect, that you may be perfect and complete, lacking in nothing."*

Chapter 27

Praise and Worship as a Weapon

I want to encourage you to view and use Praise and Worship as an act of spiritual warfare. This one act is so simple, you won't even consider it as warfare. The beauty of it is that praise can be both a defensive and offensive weapon. In the midst of it, you will begin to feel rejuvenated and strengthened. I say this, but not everyone will feel this way, and some will even shy away and pull back. I used to be one of those people.

I grew up in a denominational church where you sat quietly, we sang hymns, which I actually love hymns today, especially those where the men sing one part and then the women join in later, I can't sing at all so I was always in awe at how beautiful it sounded. Anyhow, as a kid, the service was arranged, set, and there was not a lot of room for the Holy Spirit to move in the room. Actually, I don't think the Holy Spirit was ever invited. My point is, I was conditioned, and even as an adult who is fully Holy Spirit filled, I still have some of those tendencies at times. So, praise was not something that came naturally to me. My husband on the other hand, as soon as he became Spirit filled was all about praise. He is one of those who will yell out "Amen!" when the pastor says something he likes. I think my pastor loves that. I think it perks him up mid message when someone

259

does that. He knows at least one person is listening!! Maybe you are more like me, or more demonstrative like my husband or somewhere in between. No matter, there is a way to get your praise on and do it to feel natural and grow in your relationship with the Lord that way. Did I mention the enemy hates praise? The sooner we can develop it into our daily lives, the more we are sharpening our weapons and getting the enemy to not want to be around us.

Before we look at some people in the Bible known for their praise, let's talk about praise and exactly what it is because I think a lot of times people confuse praise with worship and they are different but extremely complimentary, so they are often joined which is why some don't know the difference right away.

Think of praise as coming from our heart to the Lord. It is a heartfelt way to show love, respect, thankfulness, an emotion that can be difficult to put into words. It is our way of showing and sharing with the Lord our devotion to him. We generally use words, but it can be actions as well to express to Him our devotion.

Worship takes praise and goes further. Worship will take that praise and put it to song, put it to dance, put it into action in a way that shows a surrender to the Lord. Worship provides us the opportunity to invite the Holy Spirit into our lives at that very moment. We humble ourselves in worship because we let go of ourselves and seek Him deeper in relationship with Him. We can, at times, get overwhelmed by the Holy Spirit when we worship. So, you can see how they become joined.

In the Bible, David is probably the most famous for combining his praise of the Lord with worship. He was a musician, so it was natural for him. I play a mean triangle; I cannot sing, so it does not come naturally to me. If you ever see my husband and me in the audience of any kind of theatre musical, that's all him, I am there by duress.

Let's take a look at some of David's praise and worship. David wrote about half of the book of Psalms, he is credited with 75 of the 150. He is listed in Psalms as the author of 73, then the New Testament refers to him as the author of two additional Psalms, so 75 total. Thirteen of the Psalms David wrote had context. They were praise and worship he expressed in the midst of a trial or something specific happening at the time. The ones we will be discussing are just about praise and worship.

Let's take a look at Psalms 138:

Verse 1-3

I will praise you, Lord, with all my heart;
* before the "gods" I will sing your praise.*
2 I will bow down toward your holy temple
* and will praise your name*
* for your unfailing love and your faithfulness,*
for you have so exalted your solemn decree
* that it surpasses your fame.*
3 When I called, you answered me;
* you greatly emboldened me.*

Verse 6-8

Though I walk in the midst of trouble,
*   you preserve my life.*
You stretch out your hand against the anger of my foes;
*   with your right hand you save me.*
8 The Lord will vindicate me;
*   your love, Lord, endures forever—*
*   do not abandon the works of your hands.*

Verse 13-18

For you created my inmost being;
*   you knit me together in my mother's womb.*
14 I praise you because I am fearfully and wonderfully made;
*   your works are wonderful,*
*   I know that full well.*
15 My frame was not hidden from you
*   when I was made in the secret place,*
*   when I was woven together in the depths of the earth.*
16 Your eyes saw my unformed body;
*   all the days ordained for me were written in your book*
*   before one of them came to be.*
17 How precious to me are your thoughts,[a] God!
*   How vast is the sum of them!*
18 Were I to count them,
*   they would outnumber the grains of sand—*
*   when I awake, I am still with you.*

You can hear the praise in these words and feel his heart. Now imagine these words put to song with music. Unfortunately, we don't know today exactly how it sounded when David sang it; not all of those instruments exist today, but we can get an understanding of how David felt.

This next Psalm, I call the Praise Psalm. It's Psalm 148.

Praise the Lord.

Praise the Lord from the heavens;
  praise him in the heights above.
2 Praise him, all his angels;
  praise him, all his heavenly hosts.
3 Praise him, sun and moon;
  praise him, all you shining stars.
4 Praise him, you highest heavens
  and you waters above the skies.

5 Let them praise the name of the Lord,
  for at his command they were created,
6 and he established them for ever and ever—
  he issued a decree that will never pass away.

7 Praise the Lord from the earth,
  you great sea creatures and all ocean depths,
8 lightning and hail, snow and clouds,
  stormy winds that do his bidding,
9 you mountains and all hills,
  fruit trees and all cedars,
10 wild animals and all cattle,
  small creatures and flying birds,
11 kings of the earth and all nations,
  you princes and all rulers on earth,
12 young men and women,
  old men and children.

13 Let them praise the name of the Lord,
  for his name alone is exalted;
  his splendor is above the earth and the heavens.

14 *And he has raised up for his people a horn,*
the praise of all his faithful servants,
of Israel, the people close to his heart.

Praise the Lord.

This Psalm is all about Praising the Lord, the heavens and the earth. This one I wanted to discuss specifically because if you want something to help you in your praise, memorize these. There is something for everyone here so even if you can only remember a few of the lines, if it means something to you and it is scripture and it is praise that is a trifecta weapon against the enemy. Use it!!

You really can turn any scripture into a way to praise the Lord. Paul tells us in 2 Timothy 3:16-17, *All Scripture is God-breathed and is useful for teaching, rebuking, correcting and training in righteousness, so that the servant of God may be thoroughly equipped for every good work.* I say it's all good for praising as well. Even the shortest scripture in the Bible. Do you know what it is? It's just two words. John 11:35, *Jesus wept.* Why on earth would I consider that a praise scripture we can use as a weapon? Well, first off it has Jesus' name in it. Just saying His name is praise. Second, the enemy hates hearing the name of Jesus. Third, the enemy knows what you are referencing in this scripture. Fourth, think about the scripture. All you have to do is think about the scripture in context, and it becomes an incredibly powerful praise that should light you up and give you unending encouragement. Jesus wept because Lazarus was dead. Jesus cared for Lazarus. Jesus cares for all of us as well. We are no less important than Lazarus. What then did Jesus do? He traveled to where Lazarus lay, and He told the men there to take away the stone that was covering Lazarus' cave where his body was placed. We then read the prayer of thanksgiving Jesus gives to His Father, Our Father, and Jesus calls for Lazarus to come out and out walks Lazarus. That, my friends, is praiseworthy. "Jesus wept"

I have a friend; we have known each other, since 2008, however long that is. Anyhow, this friend has always been on fire for the Lord as long as I have known him. During this time, 2008-2009ish, we were working on projects together so we spent a lot of time together, my husband included and a few other folks. Anyhow, this friend was huge on praise. It didn't matter where we were, what we were doing, praise was coming out of his mouth, loudly, continually. If we went thirty minutes and there was no praise, we would wonder what was wrong. The first time I heard it, I didn't know how to react. I was okay with him saying it, but we were in public, and he shouted it. I knew heads turned. I just wasn't sure about it. Here's how it would go. We would be talking, ladala taldalala, then something would be said about Jesus, a testimony or a blessing being discussed. Then suddenly Tim would yell , "In the Name of Jesus!" It wasn't at the top of his lungs, but it felt pretty darn near. Over time, I grew to appreciate it and embrace it. You likely won't hear me yelling it out in public, but if you are ever in Southern California, and you hear someone yell it somewhere near you- yell out, "Tim, is that you?" Guarantee you he will respond, and you will be blessed meeting him.

Praise can be forgotten when we get into the hustle and bustle of our day. Bring it out, make time for it; it will make a difference. The Lord never fails to show when we call on Him.

Worship clearly has a place and a purpose in the time we spend with the Lord, not just at church or in our car while we drive.

Chapter 28

Fasting Creates Breakthrough

Fasting not only deepens your relationship with the Lord but also serves to counterattack the enemy's plans over you, your family, your church, your business, anywhere you are involved or have a heart to protect or build. Our discussion will center around what fasting is, how we can include that in our lives, and why we want to include it in our lives.

We are going to do things a little differently in this chapter. My book, Loving Conversations: How to Pray and Hear God's Voice, starts with a my going on a fast. So, I am going to read part of the first chapter of my book to you about that fast.

I have known the Lord all of my life. As a young girl, I remember singing the songs in Sunday school, working in little paper workbooks and hearing all about Him. At 5 or 6 years old, my grandfather sat me on his knee and transferred Godly wisdom and knowledge to me that, at the time, I did not even remotely understand, but years later flashed into my mind at the exact moment I needed it and has never left my heart. I was saved and baptized at 13, by a very large and somewhat scary German preacher in Stuttgart, Germany. I never strayed too far from the Lord as I entered adulthood. I'm a staying within the line's kind of gal. My late 20's and early 30's were filled with marriage and child rearing. My mid 30's and 40's were growth years. While I did have a good career, my relationship with the Lord grew exponentially in ways I did not know were still possible in today's modern world. He spoke to me and shared His heart with me, and I was the strongest and closer to Him than I had ever been. However, as I neared 50, I just wasn't hearing from the Lord in the same way I had for almost 20 years. In my mind, nothing had changed. I was reading the Bible, leading Bible studies, going to church, praying and trusting in the Lord, but the silence was unmistakable.

My answer, at the time, to breaking this silence was foolproof. I will fast. I will fast, not for a day or even 2 days or even 3 days, no I will fast in a way the Lord cannot help but to notice. I will complete a 21-day Daniel fast. Yes, this was definitely the answer. Whatever it is that is creating this blockage for me to hear from the Lord will have no chance against a 21-day Daniel Fast. If you aren't familiar with this Fast, it's modeled after the events described in the book of Daniel in the Bible and consists of a plant-based diet. This fast might not seem like a challenge, but for me, I might as well have been standing at the bottom of Mt. Everest looking up. Maybe that's an exaggeration, but just go with me that it was a big deal for me. My logic was simple. Breakthrough happens when you fast, and I needed breakthrough, and I needed it now.

As I prepared for the fast, I laid out my plan. I like plans and I like lists, so I was already excited just preparing in the knowledge that change was coming. I bought a new journal to document the entire event, the good, the bad, and ultimately the breakthroughs would all be documented for me to go back and review and re-experience later. I have journaled for years as a way to hear from the Lord so I wanted to be prepared for the outpouring that will surely happen in the coming days. I had 5 major areas in my life that I was seeking breakthrough. I wanted as a result to see answered prayers, blessings, favor, an outpouring in all 5 of those areas. I not only wanted it, I needed it. I had to hear what the Lord had for me, where was He, why was I struggling to hear from Him. My heart and my mind felt desperate.

I did my grocery shopping for the first week. I was very disciplined for that hour and a half in the store. I did not get anything with sugar, no breads, no pasta, I focused on vegetables and fruit. I have very few, ok, maybe no vegetables I can say I love, but there are some I do like a lot. Of course, those are prepped with bacon or some other fat that is not a part of this fast, so I was trying to develop my creativity, awaken my inner chef that I let take a few years off since the kids have grown and for the most part out of the house. Once home, I got out my containers and got everything lined up on the counter. I spent what felt like hours prepping all my veggies and fruit, trying to convince myself I was going to enjoy this change. I wanted to move forward, and this seemed like a small price to pay.

I also shored myself up mentally for the next 21 days of water. I decided to leave out tea or coffee and stick with water only knowing headaches were inevitable while going through a caffeine detox. I strongly dislike drinking water. I know people who can tell the difference in waters, brands, what mountain the waters came from, and are happy to pay a high price for their favorite water but that is not a part of who I am. The mental struggle I put myself through just thinking about drinking only water for 21 days was a little on the ridiculous side. At that time, my deepest love in a beverage was sweet tea. A love affair that admittedly still exists.

I also pulled together some books on prayer. I leaned on the works of one of the prayer greats, E.M. Bounds. I figured I might need some help with prayer and E.M. Bounds seemed like the right fit. I wanted into that "secret place" E.M. Bounds was known for and I wasn't going to stop until I got inside. Nothing was going to stop me now. I was prepped and ready to go and it all came down to one thing, the date, when would this move of my life begin. The date I chose was September 8, 2018. I want to say a "date which will live in infamy", but it wasn't quite that dramatic. I love history so forgive me now for any excessive use of historical references, it's just the way my mind thinks and tends to keep me entertained.

On September 8, 2018, I started Day One quoting E.M. Bounds in my journal. Somehow putting his words to a few pages made me feel accomplished, it was documented proof I had begun the fast after all. The depth of E.M. Bounds' words were somehow magnified as I worked through the morning trying to keep my mind off not only food, but the long 21 days ahead. On page four I began to write to the Lord, write my heart out to Him about why I began this fast. I told him that it started out as needing *breakthrough in one area but had grown and had also become about feeling lost. I wrote of how I wanted to get back to Him and His plan. I explained that somewhere along the way, what started out as a journey with Him no longer felt like we were walking together. Then I quieted myself and prepared to wait on His response. What I didn't realize in that moment was that my feeling lost, my not hearing from Him and no longer feeling like we were walking together was all **me**. It had nothing to do with Him at all.*

So that fast, that was the longest, most difficult and most rewarding fast I have ever done in my life. It changed my life. Everything in my life shifted after that fast, and it prepared me for some pretty big events I didn't know were coming. So, let's talk about fasting, who did it, why we should consider it, what it is and what it is not.

The list of people in the Bible who fasted is like looking at a Who's Who of amazing people of the Bible. Moses, David, Esther, Ezra, Daniel, Hannah- the mother of Samuel, Nehemiah, Joshua, all of the Disciples, Paul, Barnabas, the list goes on, to include Jesus. There is a reason why they all fasted and why it is included in the Bible. Anything that was done by so many of the great people we learn from in the Bible in both the Old and New Testament, is something we should examine and see how it applies to our lives today.

We are going to take a look at Jesus, when he fasted for forty days in the wilderness. This is not a fast most people are able to do; for health reasons we would definitely want to see a doctor if we were attempting something of that magnitude. We want to fast safely. We'll talk more about that in a bit, but I want to address that now to decrease any

271

concerns about that in the beginning. So, Matthew 4 tells us about Jesus' fast and here is what it says:

Then Jesus was led by the Spirit into the wilderness to be tempted by the devil. After fasting forty days and forty nights, he was hungry. The tempter came to him and said, "If you are the Son of God, tell these stones to become bread." Jesus answered, "It is written: 'Man shall not live on bread alone, but on every word that comes from the mouth of God.'" Then the devil took him to the holy city and had him stand on the highest point of the temple. "If you are the Son of God," he said, "throw yourself down. For it is written:

> *"He will command his angels concerning you,*
>   *and they will lift you up in their hands,*
>   *so that you will not strike your foot against a stone.'"*

Jesus answered him, "It is also written: 'Do not put the Lord your God to the test.'" Again, the devil took him to a very high mountain and showed him all the kingdoms of the world and their splendor. "All this I will give you," he said, "if you will bow down and worship me." Jesus said to him, "Away from me, Satan! For it is written: 'Worship the Lord your God, and serve him only.'" Then the devil left him, and angels came and attended him.

Jesus was led by the Spirit in His fast; we too can be led by the Spirit to fast, or we can seek to fast on our own. His fast was for forty days in the wilderness. Even if we were able to fast for forty days, it is not likely going to be in the wilderness of Israel, in the sun. The wilderness there is treacherous. We are likely doing it in the comfort of our homes, maybe with air conditioning, or our offices; it's not the same, and we don't need it to be the same. Satan came directly at Jesus. We likely won't have Satan coming at us, but we could have some demons. Jesus did not hesitate to respond to Satan's tactics with scripture, and untwisting the perversions Satan was applying to the Word. We have the written word readily available in most countries, so we should also be able to discern when the Word is twisted. At the end, Jesus overcame those temptations, and his ministry began. His ministry began with power and authority and miracles.

While our circumstances of our may be different from Jesus, the elements and the outcomes are the same. A fast, a heartfelt fast, will provide you with strength to endure, and you will walk out of it with much more than you walked in and may even produce power, authority and miracles in your life with Him.

So, let's dig in deeper about why we should consider it. First off, what is it exactly? We've reviewed it, but what is it exactly? Fasting is simply abstaining from, generally food, for a spiritual purpose. I say generally because we can also abstain from other things that would be acceptable for a fast, like abstaining from our phones for a period so that we can instead devote that time to the Lord.

Fasting is really meant for everyone. It is not for the spiritually mature or for only those in a ministry role. It is for all of us. Paul writes in Romans 12:1 *"Therefore, I urge you, brothers and sisters, in view of God's mercy, to offer your bodies as a living sacrifice, holy and pleasing to God—this is your true and proper worship."* So, when we are fasting, we are offering our bodies; we are making a sacrifice. Anytime we do that for the Lord when our hearts are sincere, we cannot go wrong. The Lord will honor what we are doing, even if we don't do it very well. If we are fasting and fall prey to temptation, well, get back up and try again. He never said we have to be perfect, so don't let that stop you.

273

When our heart is right, and by that I mean, our motives to fast are genuine, fasting is a source of release. There are some things, supernatural things, that can only be released through fasting. Jesus tells his disciples that when they are unable to cast a demon out. By that we know that the act of fasting produces an authority and a power we wouldn't have otherwise. What else can fasting do?

Fasting produces breakthrough

Fasting produces healing

Fasting breaks bondages

Fasting increases anointing

Fasting deepens your relationship with Him

Fasting builds desire for Him and His plan in your life

Fasting releases the power of His promises

Fasting reveals enemy tactics

Fasting breaks the cycle of religion

Fasting is not a work

Fasting provides opportunity to intercede for others

Fasting magnifies your heart

Fasting breaks strongholds

I could go on and on here, but I think you see where this all goes.

Fasting is a powerful weapon. The enemy doesn't want us to fast. He knows what happens, what can be, and what will be released when we fast.

A few things to keep in mind. Jesus tells us in Matthew 6:16, *"When you fast, do not look somber as the hypocrites do, for they disfigure their faces to show others they are fasting. Truly I tell you, they have received their reward in full. But when you fast, put oil on your head and wash your face, so that it will not be obvious to others that you are fasting, but only to your Father, who is unseen; and your Father, who sees what is done in secret, will reward you.*

This leads me to the obstacles of fasting. Most people think of the obstacles as self-control, doubt, discouragement, selfish desires, rebellion, which are all obstacles for sure - but what about pride? The Pharisees, whom the Lord called hypocrites, because they were making a show of their fast, so that everyone would know it. Their pride and arrogance made their fast null and void. Their heart was not genuine. When we fast, be discreet, and keep it private so that you are honoring the Lord. Does this mean you don't tell your spouse or those who are close enough to you that it would affect? No, if you need to share it so the ones around you understand why you have a change in behavior then do so.

One way I like to think of fasting is that I am sowing into my relationship with the Lord. I will let Him decide when and how the reaping occurs, especially if I am not fasting for myself. Now let's go through the mechanics of fasting.

You can fast for breakthrough or whatever your specific petition is for yourself. You can fast for an outcome for someone else like healing or a job. You can fast for your church. You can fast for an event, so the outcome is what the Lord wants. You can fast for a list of things. In my Twenty One Day Daniel Fast, I was praying for five specific things. That is part of the reason I chose twenty one days. I was fasting for a lot, so I wanted to put an appropriate amount of time toward my fast. There is no hard and fast rule, but I would consider how you want to proceed based on what you are seeking from the Lord.

The things I like about fasting are how versatile they can be. You can tailor them to your schedule. Maybe you fast for a certain number of hours each day. You could do every other day. You could do one day a week for several weeks. Build it to work with your schedule so you can be successful.

There are 4 basic types of fasts.

1.   Complete Fast: no food no water, this should be rare and doctor approved

2.   Normal fast: no food, just liquids

3.   Partial fast: no meat, only veggies, or time dictated

4.   Custom fast: no coffee, no soda, one meal, easier for people with health concerns

Don't forget you can do any or all of these with non-food items as well. It just needs to be something that is a sacrifice of some sort, so it is authentic.

When I did my twenty one-day Daniel fast, it changed my life. God revealed His plan and purpose for my life. During it, He gave me the Loving Conversations book, and as a result my life has never been the same. I have a new business building believers in the Kingdom. We have traveled the world for our YouTube Channel. I have a podcast, and even this book is a result of that fast. My podcast is in forty-two countries as of this writing, and I get so much feedback of how lives are changed from understanding more about how the enemy has been influencing their lives and how they are changing and growing in the Lord. I'm just one person and so much came out of one fast. What can you do to change your life or someone else's life with just one fast? It's not a work, don't see it as a works-based activity. It's a heart-based activity where you will receive more back than you will ever give up. Commit to putting it on the calendar and decide what kind of fast you are going to do, and let Him move in your life.

Chapter 29

How and Why We Use the Blood of Jesus in Our Lives

We need to discuss the blood of Jesus, and I mean to specifically understand why we plead the blood of Jesus. This is considered unbiblical by some because they accuse Christians of using the blood of Jesus like a slot machine, or even unbiblical that we claim the blood for protection because it is past, not current. When I hear that argument, I'm not convinced those who say such things understand the significance God gave the blood from the beginning. So, we are going to address this and break down how we should be using the blood of Jesus in our lives. The importance and significance of the blood from the beginning to the end of times which we see in the Book of Revelation.

As believers, we should all agree Jesus has redeemed us - meaning He paid the price for us through His sacrifice, through the shedding of His blood on the cross. He has justified us - meaning He has made us righteous through His sacrifice. That doesn't mean we are perfect, but through Him we are made righteous. He is also our Intercessor as it says it in Isaiah 53, and He tells us that no one comes to the Father except through Him which is in John. We should all be able to agree that Jesus has sanctified us, that is a word a lot of people don't like because it sounds complicated, but it really just refers to being set apart from Sin by being in relationship with Jesus. It doesn't mean we never sin, but rather Jesus forgives. We sin; we get back up, repent. It is our relationship with Him which provides us that opportunity for forgiveness. We can all agree, or we should all be able to agree on those areas as an understanding of Christianity. Where we need to spend time is on discussing the necessity of the blood and the power it does have and why we would call on that in our lives.

We are going to go through some scripture and use a lot of Old Testament references. The Old Testament gives us the base for what happens in the New Testament, so we do need to know it. The Old Testament explains the New Testament.

Let's start from the beginning. Passover. In Exodus 12 we read about the Passover. At this time the Israelites were still in Egypt; they were slaves to the Egyptians, and Moses was to lead them out, but Moses had to follow specific instructions from God on how to accomplish that successfully. God had produced several plagues at this point, and there was a judgment that was about to take place. For the Israelites, God provided protection using the blood from a sacrificial lamb. The judgment of God and the plague God was going to send over the land of Egypt was death to the firstborn of man and animal. God was redeeming the Israelites and offering life through the use of the blood of a sacrificial Lamb - if they were obedient to His instructions. Each family had to sacrifice an animal so they could have the blood they necessary to sacrifice for saving the lives of their first born. The Lamb is one of many prophetic references to Jesus. The Israelites were then given specific instructions on how to apply the sacrificial blood in verse 22. They were take the blood of the lamb which had been collected into a bason and using hyssop, which was a wild plant, they were to apply the blood to the lintel, and the side posts of their home. Then, they had to stay in their houses. They could not go outside, or they would no longer be protected from God's judgment. When the blood was seen, that house was spared. So again, God provided a way, but they had to be obedient, or they would lose their protection. If they are not protected, their firstborn children would die. In His protection is Life.

Now let's move over to Leviticus 17, the Israelites are now in the wilderness, and let's see what God tells Moses about how the priests are to operate in the tabernacle. God gave specific instructions regarding their sacrifices and in those instructions, He tells them what they are to do with the blood of the animal that is sacrificed. The priests were to sprinkle the blood of the animal on the altar. In verse 11, God tells Moses the life of the flesh is in the blood, so they are not to eat the blood. He tells them four times in that chapter alone not to eat the blood, or there will be consequences. If God is telling them this multiple times, it must be important.

Now let's go take a look at Isaiah. Isaiah has numerous prophetic words about the coming of Jesus, and we are going to take a look at a few relating to the blood. Isaiah 53 tells us a lot about God's plan for Jesus, His purpose, and what He would have to go through to fulfill that purpose.

Verse 4:

Surely he took up our pain
and bore our suffering,
yet we considered him punished by God,

281

stricken by him, and afflicted.
But he was pierced for our transgressions, (pierced on the cross, resulting
in blood poured out)
  he was crushed for our iniquities;
the punishment that brought us peace was on him,
  and by his wounds we are healed. (referencing blood)
We all, like sheep, have gone astray,
  each of us has turned to our own way;
and the Lord has laid on him
  the iniquity of us all.

He was oppressed and afflicted,
  yet he did not open his mouth;
he was led like a lamb to the slaughter, (blood of the lamb, He is the
Lamb)
  and as a sheep before its shearers is silent,
  so he did not open his mouth.
By oppression and judgment he was taken away.
  Yet who of his generation protested?
For he was cut off from the land of the living; (death)
  for the transgression of my people he was punished.
He was assigned a grave with the wicked,
  and with the rich in his death,
though he had done no violence,
  nor was any deceit in his mouth.

Yet it was the Lord's will to crush him and cause him to suffer,
  and though the Lord makes his life an offering for sin, (Atonement)
he will see his offspring and prolong his days,
  and the will of the Lord will prosper in his hand.
After he has suffered,
  he will see the light of life and be satisfied; (the resurrection, life)
by his knowledge my righteous servant will justify many,
  and he will bear their iniquities.

Therefore I will give him a portion among the great,
*   and he will divide the spoils with the strong,*
because he poured out his life unto death,
*   and was numbered with the transgressors.*
For he bore the sin of many,
*   and made intercession for the transgressors. (Intercessor)*

If we look at what occurred in Exodus, what the priests were required to do in Leviticus, and what we just read in Isaiah, we can clearly see that the blood in each case represented life. Think about this, when God used Mary to give us Jesus, He used his own blood, His own flesh to create Jesus. Jesus wasn't created out of nothing; He was created out of the life of God combined with what He required of Mary to give us Jesus. God combined His deity with Mary's humanity to give us Jesus. Now let's take that a step further.

In John 6, starting with verse 31 we see Jesus giving us an understanding of life and an explanation of Old Testament references and prophecy.

Our ancestors ate the manna in the wilderness; as it is written: 'He gave them bread from heaven to eat.'" Jesus said to them, "Very truly I tell you, it is not Moses who has given you the bread from heaven, but it is my Father who gives you the true bread from heaven. For the bread of God is the bread that comes down from heaven and gives life to the world." "Sir," they said, "always give us this bread." Then Jesus declared, "I am the bread of life. Whoever comes to me will never go hungry, and whoever believes in me will never be thirsty. But as I told you, you have seen me and still you do not believe. All those the Father gives me will come to me, and whoever comes to me I will never drive away. For I have come down from heaven not to do my will but to do the will of him who sent me. And this is the will of him who sent me, that I shall lose none of all those he has given me, but raise them up at the last day. For my Father's will is that everyone who looks to the Son and believes in him shall have eternal life, and I will raise them up at the last day."

At this the Jews there began to grumble about him because he said, "I am the bread that came down from heaven." They said, "Is this not Jesus, the son of Joseph, whose father and mother we know? How can he now say, 'I came down from heaven'?" "Stop grumbling among yourselves," Jesus answered. "No one can come to me unless the Father who sent me draws them, and I will raise them up at the last day. It is written in the Prophets: 'They will all be taught by God.' Everyone who has heard the Father and learned from him comes to me. No one has seen the Father except the one who is from God; only he has seen the Father. Very truly I tell you, the one who believes has eternal life. I am the bread of life. Your ancestors ate the manna in the wilderness, yet they died. But here is the bread that comes down from heaven, which anyone may eat and not die. I am the living bread that came down from heaven. Whoever eats this bread will live forever. This bread is my flesh, which I will give for the life of the world."

Then the Jews began to argue sharply among themselves, "How can this man give us his flesh to eat?" Jesus said to them, "Very truly I tell you, unless you eat the flesh of the Son of Man and drink his blood, you have no life in you. Whoever eats my flesh and drinks my blood has eternal life, and I will raise them up at the last day. For my flesh is real food and my blood is real drink. Whoever eats my flesh and drinks my blood remains in me, and I in them. Just as the living Father sent me and I live because of the Father, so the one who feeds on me will live because of me. This is the bread that came down from heaven. Your ancestors ate manna and died, but whoever feeds on this bread will live forever."

Understand we do this to be in communion with Him, not as a memorial to Him. We don't do communion as a sad, somber event, it is a joyous time to proclaim our life in Him.

284

1 Corinthians 11:23 says this: *For I received from the Lord what I also passed on to you: The Lord Jesus, on the night he was betrayed, took bread, and when he had given thanks, he broke it and said, "This is my body, which is for you; do this in remembrance of me." In the same way, after supper he took the cup, saying, "This cup is the new covenant in my blood; do this, whenever you drink it, in remembrance of me." For whenever you eat this bread and drink this cup, you proclaim the Lord's death until he comes.*

When we take communion, we do it because we are saved. An unsaved person does not participate in communion - they should not. It is not appropriate to do so. If Jesus is not your Savior, an act to symbolize communion with Him has no meaning. It's important to understand that from God's point of view - life is in the blood and the blood is in the flesh. When we partake of communion, we are taking part in the flesh and blood of Jesus, we spiritually become a part of Him. It was God's plan from the beginning. It is in the Bible from the beginning. It's also in the Bible at the end. Let's look at the Book of Revelation 12:10. The event described here takes place in the future, end times where there is a war in heaven and Satan gets thrown down. Here is what John describes next:

Then I heard a loud voice in heaven say:

"Now have come the salvation and the power
  and the kingdom of our God,
  and the authority of his Messiah.
For the accuser of our brothers and sisters,
  who accuses them before our God day and night,
  has been hurled down.
They triumphed over him

by the blood of the Lamb
and by the word of their testimony;

Here we see the victory for Jesus is accomplished through
His blood.

I know that was a lot of information to absorb, but are you
hearing a theme? The blood offers us life. The blood is life.
The blood has power and the authority of Jesus. And it is
how, in the end, we overcome Satan. The blood is important.
The blood is biblical, and we are both able and expected to
use it to overcome the enemy.

The next question naturally is then where and how do we use
it? Well, we need to understand that the use of the blood
must coincide with the will of God, so we must be aligned
with God. If we try to use it for selfish motives, it won't
work. When it aligns with His plans, then it most certainly
will work.

Going back to my son's story, the night we had to rush back
to the hospital, I used the blood of Jesus to ensure my son's
life was protected. I knew what we were being told by the
doctors did not line up with the word the Lord gave me
about the situation. Anything contrary to His word could not
be the truth of God. The doctor's words could not be his
outcome because God said he would recover which means he
will live.

After rushing back to the hospital and I walked in the room
to see him, my son looked lifeless laying there. It was heart
wrenching, but I didn't have time to deal with my heart. I had
to use my head to pray and plead the blood of Jesus over my
son. My son has accepted Jesus as His savior, so he had a

right to His lifesaving blood. What the Lord says is the only truth in this situation. No matter how things looked or how I felt by what I saw. The Lord said my son would recover and that is what I chose to put my faith in, the words of the Lord.

Knowing my son's life was in alignment with what the Lord told me, I knew pleading the blood was the right prayer; the right words to use. We need to make sure we are in alignment and that our ask is in alignment with Him. If you can't hear God speak to you, then pray the character of who God is and seek His will in the situation. We don't pray and use His blood lightly. We pray and plead the blood when we need protection, when we are facing something that we need His life blood to intervene. The enemy cannot stand against the blood. Today I heard someone say they used to plead the blood in prayer, but they heard a demon tell them the blood of Jesus doesn't work. So, they never said it again. This person then went on to chastise anyone who did use the blood, stating that it doesn't work, as if they were an authority on it. That's stupidity. Of course, the enemy will tell you it doesn't work. He is a liar. If the enemy can convince you praying the blood doesn't work, you will stop using it in your prayer life. Can we refer back to Revelation 12;11? It tells us the enemy was conquered by the blood of the Lamb! Nough said!!!

Chapter 30

Final Thoughts

If you have arrived here because you have read the whole book, then we have spent a lot of time together now, and I hope you are encouraged to spend time in the Word, in prayer and in building your relationship with the Lord. We have only one way to *Conquer Our Unseen Enemies*, and that is through the relationship we have with Jesus and the blood He shed for us all.

If you are on this page because you want to see how it ends, guess what, He already won and so have we!! Now go back and read the rest of the book like the other folks ☺

Don't let the time you have invested here go to waste. Take what you need from this and apply it to your life and start to fulfill your purpose in the Kingdom. The biggest regret I hear from people every week is how much they have let themselves get in their own way by not being obedient to the call from the Holy Spirit. Move toward Him as you begin your journey of *Conquering Our Unseen Enemies.*

Take a look at Dawn's other books:

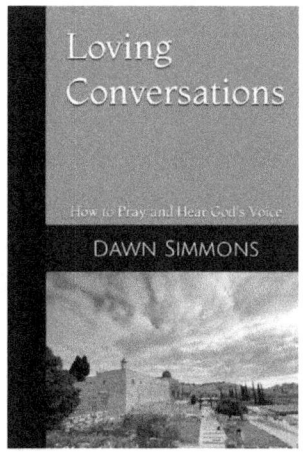

Loving Conversations: How to Pray and Hear God's Voice
ISBN: 9781960775054

Loving Conversations: Study Guide and Journal
ISBN: 9781960775061

God's Promises SALO Devotional (for women)
ISBN: 9781960775078

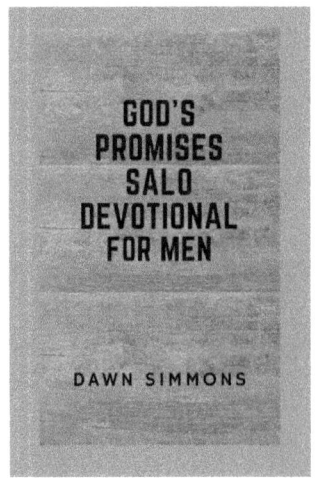

God's Promises SALO Devotional for Men
ISBN: 9781960775085